Tokyo Outdoors

45 WALKS, HIKES AND CYCLING ROUTES
TO EXPLORE THE CITY LIKE A LOCAL

Matthew Baxter

Help spread the word

Please help this self-published book by writing a review online, sharing the book on Facebook or Instagram, or telling a friend. As this is a self-funded indie project, it would be super useful and very much appreciated!

Like or follow me to get the latest tips and deals

 www.supercheapjapan.com

 @SuperCheapJapan

 @SuperCheapJapan

#TokyoOutdoors

Copyright © 2023 by Matthew Baxter

All rights reserved. No part of this publication may be reproduced, distributed or transmitted in any form or by any means, including photocopying, recording, or other electronic or mechanical methods, without the prior written permission of the publisher, except in the case of brief quotations embodied in critical reviews and certain other noncommercial uses permitted by copyright law. For permission requests, write to the publisher, addressed "Attention: Permissions Coordinator," at the address below.

Super Cheap Japan
9 Eashing Lane, Godalming, Surrey GU7 2JZ
www.supercheapjapan.com/contact/

Book Layout ©2023 BookDesignTemplates.com

Ordering Information:
Special discounts are available on quantity purchases by corporations, associations, and others. For details, contact the "Special Sales Department" at the address above.

Tokyo Outdoors: 45 Walks, Hikes and Cycling Routes to Explore the City Like a Local / Matthew Baxter — 1st ed. (IngramSpark paperback edition)
Paperback ISBN 978-1-9196315-5-4

Contents

Welcome to Tokyo 3
    Quick and easy ways to select your walk, ride or hike 4
    About the online maps in this book 4
    Essential information before you start 5
    Getting around Tokyo on the train 6
    Cycling in Tokyo 7

Central Tokyo 8
    The best of Tokyo's youth culture – Shibuya to Harajuku 8
    All sides of the valley – Shibuya 10
    Not just Senso-ji – Asakusa 12
    Crossing the Rainbow Bridge – Odaiba 14
    Shinkansen, characters and ramen – Tokyo Station area 16
    Shinjuku's skyscraper district – Nishi-Shinjuku 18
    Exploring Tokyo's Korea Town – Shin-Okubo 20
    Tokyo's central Olympic area – Shinjuku to Akasaka 22
    The gateway to Hibiya Park – Minato City 24
    Tokyo's stylish catwalk – Daikanyama 26
    Checking out Tokyo's cool canals – Shinagawa 28
    Transit time adventures – Haneda Airport 30
    Taking the Sumida River to the Skytree – Oji to Oshiage 32
    Ueno Park to Yanaka Ginza – Ueno and Nippori 34
    Nerding out for the day – Akihabara 36
    From the heights of money to the heights of power – Akasaka, Roppongi and the National Diet 38
    That other big terminal on the Yamanote Line - Ikebukuro 40
    From granny's Harajuku to milky hot springs - Sugamo 42
    Tokyo's essential art and museum walk – Roppongi 44
    Upmarket and historic shopping heaven – Ginza 46
    The royal circuit – Tokyo Imperial Palace 49
    Tokyo's best cherry blossom stroll – Meguro River 50

Out in the Tokyo suburbs 52
    Exploring the posh side of Tokyo – Jiyugaoka 52
    Akihabara for Japan travel addicts – Nakano 54
    Jindai Botanical Gardens – Chofu 55

Cycling the Tamagawa River – Kawasaki to Haijima 56

Ikegami's temples – Ota City 58

East Tokyo's underappreciated tourist spots – Koto City 60

Nostalgia on Edogawa River – Shibamata 62

Showa Kinen Park – Tachikawa 64

Little America – Fussa 66

Cycling Shakujii River – Oji to Itabashi 67

When Tokyo really doesn't feel like a city – Machida 68

Tokyo side trips 70
Japan's biggest Chinatown – Yokohama 70

Yokohama's foreign streets from years gone by – Yamate 72

Hiking the mysterious Takinoo Path – Nikko 74

Exploring Kamakura by bicycle – Kamakura 76

Kamakura's island of power spots – Enoshima 78

Exploring Kanto's top resort town by bicycle – Karuizawa 80

The lost railway – Karuizawa's Apt Road 82

Hachioji Castle Ruins – Hachioji (near Mount Takao) 83

Hiking into the clouds – Mount Oyama 85

Mount Nokogiri – Boso Peninsula, Chiba 88

Odawara Castle and the power of the Triforce – Odawara 89

Izu Panorama Park – Izu Peninsula 91

Top walks for your interests 92
Most popular – great for tourists new to Tokyo 92

Cherry blossoms (sakura) 92

Autumn leaves (kouyou) 93

Shopping 93

Art and museums 93

History and culture 94

Day hikes 94

Long cycling rides 94

Festival and events calendar 95
Index 97
Many thanks for reading 103
Useful Japanese for traveling 104
Other books written by Matthew Baxter 105
About the Author 105

Welcome to Tokyo

The capital city of Japan is surely one of the most exciting cities in the world, a wonderful mixture of modernity and tradition. With a population of more than 35 million in the greater Tokyo region, it's known as a 'city of cities', and each has its own flavors. One moment you'll be seeking harmony in an ancient shrine, another nerding out in Akihabara, and another cycling alongside a peaceful river. Whether you are here just for a short holiday, or staying for years, Tokyo Outdoors will enable you to immerse yourself properly in the magic of Tokyo.

This guide is not your average travel book. After living in Tokyo for many years and having written several books and countless articles about the capital, plus walked, hiked and cycled countless hours across it, I have put together custom routes for all sorts of likes and interests. The emphasis of this book is interesting tours throughout and around the city, via not just the must-see attractions but also hidden spots that only locals know. Along the way your path will be enhanced with fascinating historical, cultural and architectural highlights.

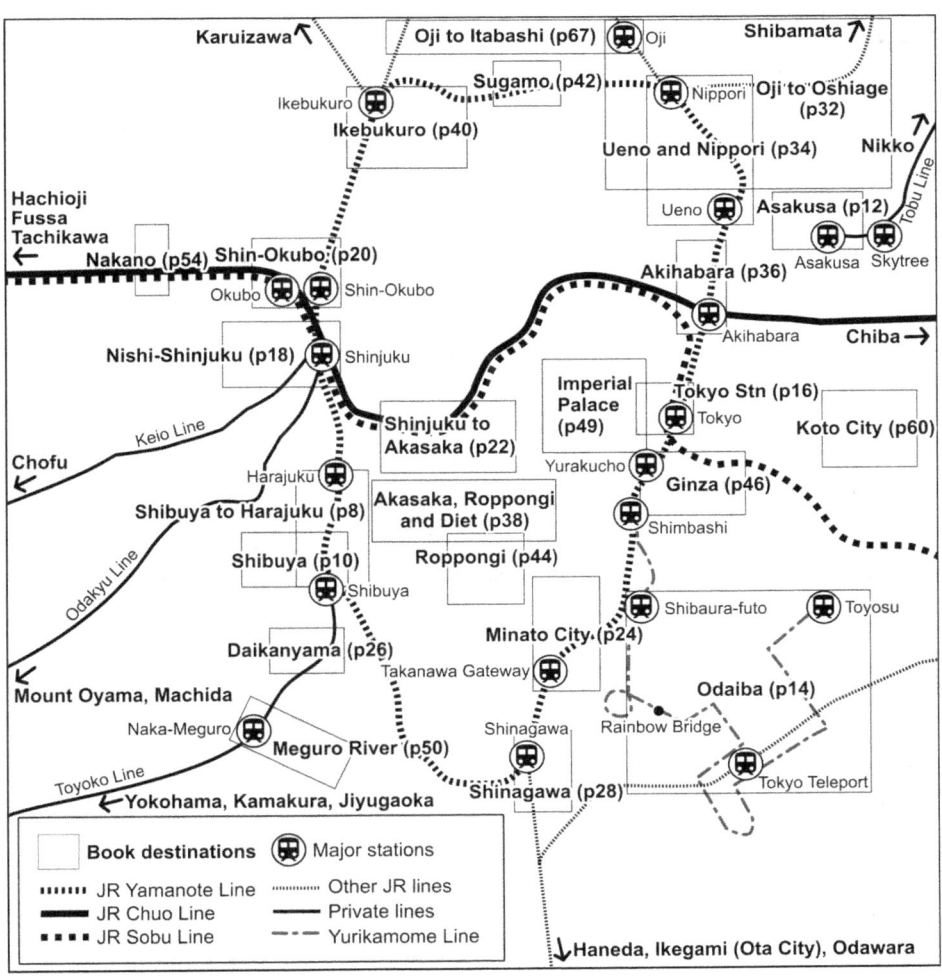

Quick and easy ways to select your walk, ride or hike

1) Tokyo city map
Use the map (p3) to get your bearings, and see what routes are near your hotel or house. It'll provide ideas if you want to walk or cycle on a certain train line, plus a good overview of what places are near to each other.

2) Top walks, hikes and cycling rides (p92)
At the back of the book is a ranking of the most popular routes, plus suggestion lists for cherry blossoms, autumn colors, shopping, art and museums, history and culture, day hikes and long cycling rides.

3) Festivals and events calendar (p95)
Tokyo has frequent festivals and events, so if you would like to experience them alongside a walk, hike or cycling ride I have put together a handy calendar.

4) Chapter suggestions
Below the title of each chapter is a little hint, such as when to do the route, or if it's best to cycle, walk or hike. Additionally, combinations are suggested for many chapters.

5) Get in touch with me
Send me an email via matt@supercheapjapan.com, or message me on Instagram or Facebook via my Super Cheap Japan pages. I'll help you out with a personal suggestion!

About the online maps in this book

supercheapjapan.com/tomaps

Most of the routes in this book also come with custom Google Maps, which can be opened on your smartphone or PC. They provide more detail on the routes and highlights along the way, plus additional recommendations for shops, cafes and tourist attractions that I will update when any changes occur. Use them with the GPS function on your phone to make navigating a breeze.

You can open them by scanning the QR code on the map in each chapter. You can also use the QR code and link above to access them all in one list, which you can save for quick access later.

Free wi-fi is available at many spots in Tokyo if you want to access the online maps, but I would recommend getting internet access on your phone in Japan if you don't already have it. Visitors can pick up a reasonably priced data SIM or a wi-fi box from the airports or at electronics stores in the city, such as Bic Camera or Yamada Denki.

Map legend

 Main spots and attractions   **Restaurants**   **Cafes and snack spots**

 Train stations   **Bus stops**   **Bicycles for rent**   **Cherry blossoms**

Essential information before you start

Train passes
If you plan to do more than one chapter from this book on your trip, or plan to venture outside the city center, it'll probably save you money to get one of the below rail passes.

Tokyo Subway Ticket (foreign tourists only)
Unlimited use of the Tokyo Metro and Toei Subway for 24, 48 or 72 hours. With this pass you'll be able to get to almost all the central Tokyo spots in this book.
800/1200/1500 yen • Available from tourist information centers in and outside of subway stations, major hotels and Bic Camera stores

One-day subway passes (all passports)
Tokyo Metro and Toei Subway also have passes for 24 hours of unlimited use of their respective networks. If you only need to use one of them, it's cheaper than the above.
Tokyo Metro 600 yen, Toei Subway 700 yen, combo pass 900 yen • Available from ticket machines at subway stations in Tokyo

Tokyo Wide Pass (non-Japanese passports only)
Unlimited use of JR trains in Tokyo and the Kanto region, for three consecutive days. As JR is the main rail provider, you can get to spots in the city center via the Yamanote loop line and other connecting lines, and the pass includes use of the Shinkansen and Limited Express trains.
   For the Tokyo side trips section (p70) of this book, it's perfect for Karuizawa (p80) and the nearby Apt Road (p82), Odawara Castle (p89), Mount Nokogiri (p88), Hachioji Castle Ruins (p83), Nikko (p74), and the Yokohama paths (p70, p72). Some might need to use a slightly longer route, or short supplementary ride on a non-JR line, but you should save lots of money!
15,000 yen • Available from the vending machines and service centers at the major JR stations in Tokyo (including Ueno, Shinjuku, Shibuya, Tokyo and Ikebukuro)

Enoshima Kamakura Free Pass
If you are doing the walk in Enoshima (p76) - and/or the cycling ride in Kamakura (p78) - then this one-day pass will cut out lots of hassle. It could also save you some money, especially if you need to additionally use the Enoden Line tram to reach, say, your hotel or hostel.
1640 yen • Available from the vending machines and the service center at the Odakyu section of Shinjuku Station in Tokyo

A note about opening days
Many shops and tourist spots are closed on Mondays or Tuesdays. In most cases, if a national holiday falls on a day when a place is usually closed, then on this day it will open, but will close on the following day. Most attractions are also closed around New Year, so I would avoid these days or check official websites to confirm if they have decided to open or not.

Useful apps to use with this book
- Google Maps, then use your wi-fi to download the areas you'll be visiting for offline use.
- Google Translate. Use it to translate text in real time via your phone's camera, which is convenient in restaurants, cafes and for Japanese signage on walking and hiking paths.
- Japan Connected-Free Wifi, to easily find free wifi spots.
- Tokyo Subway Navigation, the official app for navigating the Tokyo Metro.

Getting around Tokyo on the train

Tokyo, and the surrounding Kanto region, has a highly developed railway and subway system, so all the routes in this book begin and end at a station. Trains tend to be on schedule, often to the second, and at central stations there are departures as quick as every few minutes or so.

There are two subway networks, the Tokyo Metro and Toei Subway, plus the national operator Japan Railways (JR) and private ones such as Odakyu and Tokyu. Most are connected by the Yamanote Line, the JR line that loops around central Tokyo. It might become difficult to navigate the various options, so use the tips below to help you on your journeys.

Airport transportation

From Narita Airport, Airport Bus TYO-NRT runs 1000 yen buses into the city (1 hour), and there are also Keisei line trains to Nippori, which is on the Yamanote loop line. If coming or leaving from the more central Haneda Airport, either take the Keikyu Line to Shinagawa or the Tokyo Monorail to Hamamatsucho, both of which are on the Yamanote Line. This book also has a handy walking path if you have some transit time at Haneda (p30).

IC cards

When you arrive in Tokyo, one of the first things you should do is get an IC card. These prepaid passes can be used for public transport, plus in many shops and restaurants. The two main IC cards, Suica from JR and Pasmo from Tokyo Metro, both work on any network in Tokyo.

Cards can be purchased from ticket machines, where money can also be added to cards. Note that prices are also a little cheaper with IC cards, and that foreign tourists can get a 'Welcome Suica' card from JR Travel Service Centers, which doesn't require a deposit.
1000 yen (500 yen deposit, 500 yen put on card) • Welcome Suica card 1000 yen (no deposit)

Custom subway map for your walks and cycling routes

The official subway map can be rather overwhelming, so on the back cover of this book I have included a simplified map, highlighting the stations that you'll likely use. Full maps are also available for free at Tokyo Metro stations.

Planning your train journeys

Deciding how to get to places in Tokyo can be rather confusing at times, even for people living here. Google Maps usually works well for deciding which train to take, but doesn't include many options that help if you have a rail pass. If you want to customize your route more use the Japan Transit Planner by Jorudan, available online and as a smartphone app.

Train travel tips when using this book

- Which exit to take is included in the text and map of each route when there is more than one. Follow signage from the station platforms to the exit, but don't be afraid to ask someone if you are lost in a bigger station. Japanese people are often very willing to help!
- Subway and JR stations and lines have now been designated with simple codes to help with navigation. They use a letter or two for the line, and a number for the station, such as JY17 for Shinjuku Station on the Yamanote Line.
- I've designed the routes in the book so that many end or start near to one another. This enables you to easily join routes together, and save money on transportation. Look for 'Combine with....' sections at the end of applicable chapters for my suggestions.

Cycling in Tokyo

Hello Cycling and NTT bicycles

While most tourists prefer to use the subway, riding a bicycle can be a fun way to explore the city, and the suburbs, in more depth. You'll end up stumbling upon a few surprises as you see Japanese people in everyday life, plus you'll be able to quickly pop into quieter shrines, temples and other interesting spots that you'll come across.

There are two main bicycle rental systems in Tokyo and the surrounding Kanto region, Hello Cycling and NTT Docomo Bike Share. There are areas where only one of the systems has 'bicycle stations', but in the city center you'll probably have a choice. Convenient locations for these are shown on the maps in this book, including on the Google Maps that are linked to, but always use the official apps to check availability, and reserve your bike.

Hello Cycling

An excellent, easy to use system that generally appeals more to day trippers. While not the most extensive of systems when compared to some cities across the world, their bicycles are a good size for adults, sturdy and also have little motors if you want a boost on challenging uphill sections. All in all, it's a really impressive system.

There are a few ways to pay, including using a credit card (most foreign cards work fine). Doing the 12-hour pass with Hello Cycling is perfect for one of the longer rides in this book, and it's usually possible to reserve bikes 30 minutes in advance. Download the Hello Cycling app on your phone to find, reserve and return your bike.

12-hour pass 1200-1800 yen, or from 100 yen for first 15 minutes, then 130 yen per 30 minutes

NTT Docomo Bike Share

NTT's bicycle system has more rental points, particularly in the city center, so is often used by workers in the city to get around. One notable failing, though, is that the bikes have small wheels, with a frame that is almost as small as a portable bicycle. They are therefore not as comfortable to use as the ones from Hello Cycling, and I would not recommend them for longer routes.

Having said this, NTT Docomo Bike Share can be a little cheaper on a day pass, and there is more chance that the stations you start at will have available bikes, or the station you want to end up at will have space to park your bike. Head to https://docomo-cycle.jp to get started.

Day passes 1650 yen, or first 30 minutes 165 yen, then 165 yen every additional 30 minutes

A note about cycling in the city

Some of the main tourist spots in central Tokyo can get extremely crowded, and may have narrow streets packed with tourists. In these places it would be much easier, and safer to walk. When it's not a good idea to cycle somewhere, I have included a recommendation to walk the route at the top of each chapter.

Central Tokyo

The best of Tokyo's youth culture – Shibuya to Harajuku
DISTANCE: 3 KM | BEST ON FOOT DUE TO CROWDED STREETS

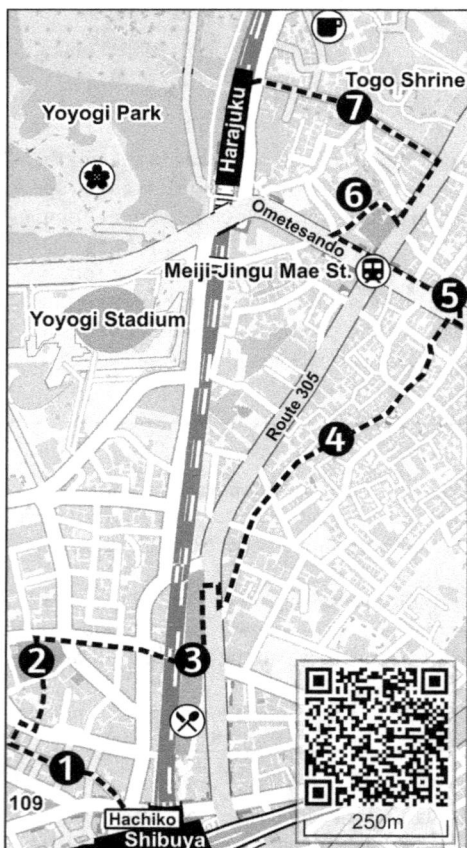

Shibuya and Harajuku are the first ports of call for most to Tokyo, and for good reason. A treasure trove of youth fashion, music and art, you'll often see trends getting big here years before they make the big time abroad.

Starting and ending points
From Shibuya Station, follow signs to the Hachiko statue to begin. Shibuya has a plethora of lines, such as the JR Yamanote and JR Shonan-Shinjuku lines, plus the Ginza, Hanzomon and Fukutoshin lines on the Tokyo Metro. You'll finish at Harajuku Station.

Places of interest

1) Shibuya Center Gai
Head across the famous **Shibuya Scramble Crossing** and you'll get to the youth hub that is Center Gai. Bustling and exciting 24 hours of the day, with young people showing off the latest designs and brands, you'll really feel like you've landed in modern Japan. While chains are somewhat on the rise here, you'll still come across plenty of eccentric little shops and some down-to-earth eateries.

2) Shibuya Parco
Much of this Parco department store has your standard collections of brand stores and fashion boutiques, but the bottom and sixth floors are where things get different. In the basement is the Chaos Kitchen food hall. Rather than the usual upmarket and safe selections of most department store food courts, this one is full of quirky bars and restaurants. Most unique is **Kome To Circus** (12am-10:30pm, from 5pm on Thursdays), an izakaya where you can try out insects, crocodile meat and other left-field options.
    Upstairs on the sixth floor is **Cyberspace Shibuya**, where the main hitters are the **Nintendo Tokyo** store (11am-8pm) and the **Pokemon Center** (11am-9pm). Whether you're a Pikachu fanboy or can't get enough of Animal Crossing, there's a real smorgasbord of amazing character goods. Even if you're just window shopping, it's worth heading up here to soak in all the craziness!
11am-9pm

3) Miyashita Park
One of the newest developments in Shibuya. Here visitors can relax in the greenery of the rooftop garden and enjoy a bit of shopping at

dozens of up-and-coming stores, as well as flagship shops for brands like Adidas.

Outside on the first floor is **Shibuya Yokocho** (24h), a line of classic Japanese street food outlets, all specializing in local food from a particular region or city in Japan. It's also a great place to try out Japanese sake and shochu (a traditional hard liquor), with English menus usually on hand.
8am-11pm

4) Cat Street
Generally catering to an older audience than the upcoming Takeshita Street, Cat Street is a hipster's paradise. Here you'll find plenty of edgy and up-and-coming boutiques, vintage clothes stores and the odd street art to admire along the way. It's a much more interesting way to journey from Shibuya to Harajuku.

5) Omotesando Hills
A super posh shopping complex designed by the renowned Tadao Ando. Inside you'll come across famous overseas labels as well as stores from local designers like Yohji Yamamoto and Jun Hashimoto. To be honest, as there aren't many around, it's also a perfect toilet stop on this walk!
11am-11pm (some shops may close earlier)

6) Ota Memorial Museum of Art
Pop in here if you need a little respite from all the activity outdoors. This museum is dedicated to the Japanese art of ukiyo-e, a kind of Japanese woodblock print. Most famous is the Thirty-six Views of Mt. Fuji, an often reproduced print of huge waves with Mount Fuji in the background. This piece has itself been on display here in the ever-changing exhibitions. Check ukiyoe-ota-muse.jp for what's on when you are in town.
Exhibits 800-1200 yen • 10:30am-5:30pm • Closed on Mondays (except national holidays)

7) Takeshita Street
Harajuku's busiest fashion street, this is the place to experience kawaii (cute) on hyperdrive! There's a seemingly countless assortment of bright and colorful shops to venture into.

There are a few highlights to look out for. First on your path will be **SoLaDo** (10:30am-8:30pm), a hotspot for kawaii souvenirs from the likes of PINK-latte and Line Friends. There's also **Sweets Paradise** (11am-9pm, 2000-3000 yen), which offers all-you-can-eat candy and dessert extravaganzas.

Further on up, **Strawberry Fetish** (9am-8pm, around 700 yen) is all the rage with its sweet strawberry sticks, but a visit to Takeshita Street is incomplete without checking out **Harajuku Alta** (10:30am-8pm). Since launching in 2015 this mall has become a new icon of Harajuku, packed with any kind of item related to Harajuku's pop culture. It's all very cute, and quite often cheap!

Recommended cafe
Would you like to get your coffee served through a hole in the wall by a furry bear? Anakuma is a kawaii coffee shop and yet another unusual addition to Harajuku. To order at this 'unmanned' joint, use the tablet and one of the seven bears that lives behind the wall will soon be ready with your coffee!
Drinks 1200-1500 yen • 11am-7pm

Recommended meal spot
At Eggslut, the humble egg is taken to new levels. Served in brioche buns, their egg burgers ooze with the creamy scrambled egg and cheese. The Japan-only limited edition specials are pretty inventive too, such as putting a whole eel into a sandwich.
From 850 yen • 11am-9pm

Shibuya Scramble Crossing

All sides of the valley – Shibuya

DISTANCE: 2.5 KM | BEST ON FOOT DUE TO CROWDED STREETS

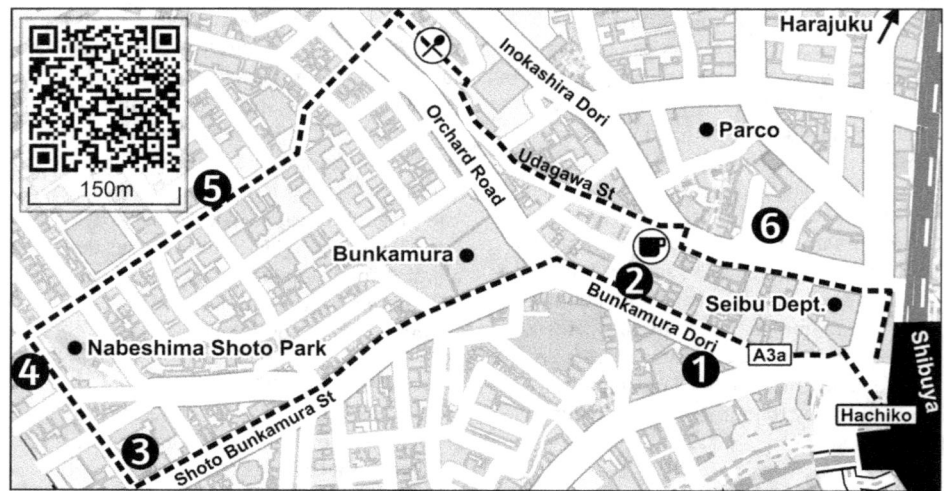

Shibuya might be most famous for the scramble crossing, but it has so much more to offer. This route will take you via the main commercial roads, then out to the suburbs to experience some museums and world-class curry cuisine that few foreign tourists reach.

Starting and ending points

Head out of Shibuya Station at the Hachiko Exit or Exit A3a, whichever is closer. From here walk up Bunkamura Dori Street to begin the walk. The route then rings round back to the station.

Places of interest

1) Shibuya 109
Known as Shibuya's fashion landmark, 109 is a high-rise mall with a wide selection of Japanese brand clothing, cosmetics and accessories. All styles are on offer, from goth to posh, and the mall is always full of youngsters looking to jump on, or start, the latest trends. Even if you are not up for buying such items, it's an enjoyable bit of window shopping, as well as a kind of cultural insight into youth culture in Japan.
10am-9pm

2) MEGA Don Quijote
The largest Don Quijote in the capital. Thousands upon thousands of random goods, from a grocery section brimming with nutty Japanese snacks to a cosmetics section that has become popular with tax-free loving tourists from south-east Asia. On the first floor you'll definitely sense the irresistible smell of **10 YEN Pancake** (actually costing 500 yen!). Round sponge cakes filled with stretchy cheese, they have become quite the in thing.
24h

Shibuya fashion is everywhere!

The Moyai Statue outside Shibuya Station

3) The Shoto Museum of Art
This first stop for culture vultures will surely come as a welcome escape from the hustle and bustle of downtown Shibuya. Located in a quiet residential area, this small museum houses centuries old paintings and sculptures. Recent exhibitions have included Okinawan textiles (Japan's southern islands), Buddhist art in Shibuya and Ainu clothing (Hokkaido's indigenous people).

In addition to the main galleries, the **Salon Exhibition** area showcases artists from or who have ties to Shibuya, so make sure you don't miss out on that too.
Exhibitions around 1000 yen • 9am-5pm • Closed on Mondays (except national holidays)

4) Gallery TOM
This gallery is not your everyday experience. Here you enjoy art through touch, rather than by sight. Founded by parents of a visually impaired child, the gallery invites artists to create sculptures and statues for visitors to literally wrap their hands around.
Entry usually 600 yen • 11am-8pm • Closed on Mondays (except national holidays)

5) Toguri Museum
A highly acclaimed museum showing off porcelain artworks. The exhibits are from the almost 10,000 strong collection of Tohru Toguri, a local collector who wanted to preserve and display Asian artwork, which he felt was fading after the postwar influx of Western culture. Inside it's not just local pieces though, with artifacts from China, Korea and Hizen (in the Arita region in southern Japan). English language tours are occasionally available, so ask at the reception if you are interested.
Exhibitions 1000-1200 yen • 10am-5pm (until 9pm on Fridays and Saturdays) • Closed on Mondays (except national holidays)

6) Shibuya Loft
More upmarket than Don Quijote, this variety store is a neat spot for gift shopping. There are also lots of handy 'only in Japan' devices that you'll want to take home as well.
10:30am-5:30pm

Recommended cafe
Become a 'Master' or 'Princess' at the Maidreamin maid cafe. The maids here perform little magic spells on your food, put on shows and serve you food shaped like cute animals. Very kawaii!
Cover charge 500 yen, food around 1000 yen • 11:30am-11pm

Recommended meal spot
A Michelin-awarded curry restaurant on the second floor of a nondescript apartment building? Yes, that's right. Pork Vindaloo Taberu Fukudaitoryo serves a Japanese take on the pork vindaloo, from Goa, India. There's always a line, and for good reason.
1000 yen • 11:30am-9pm (Closed on Sunday)

Combine with...
Once you are done with this walk, you could then continue up north to Harajuku (p8). It'll allow you to see more of Shibuya, as well as the host of less corporate and more independently owned businesses in between.

Cheap snacks and more at Don Quijote

Not just Senso-ji – Asakusa

DISTANCE: 3.5 KM | BEST ON FOOT

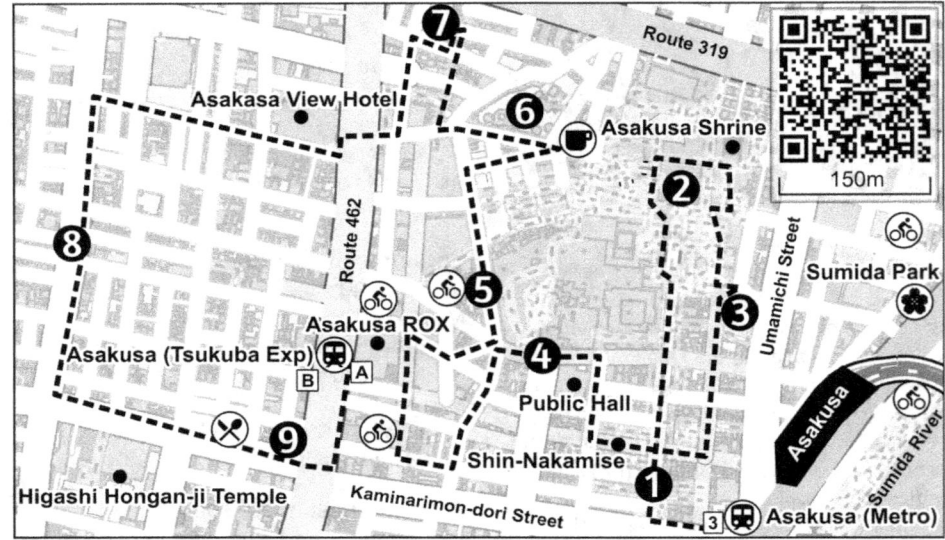

You've all heard about Asakusa, the most popular, and the busiest tourist destination in Tokyo. Millions visit Senso-ji temple and shop up Nakamise-dori every year, but there is so much more to see if you venture out a bit....

Starting and ending points

Head out from the Tokyo Metro section of Asakusa Station (Exit 3). You could either finish at Tsukuba Express Line's Asakusa Station, which goes to Akihabara, or continue back down Kaminarimon-dori back to the Tokyo Metro Asakusa Station.

Places of interest

1) Nakamise-dori Street

Let's tick off the main tourist spots before we start our real adventure (try to start early if you can, to avoid the tour groups). Beginning at **Kaminarimon Gate**, this lively shopping street has a nice mix of souvenir shops, food stalls and craft shops. Keep an eye on your wallet though, as prices will generally be better once you head out of this touristy street.

2) Senso-ji

The legend goes that two fishermen caught a golden statue in Sumida River. Even though they tried to return it to the river again and again, they kept on catching it instead. Once it was recognized as Kannon, a Buddhist deity, though, it was enshrined at this site.

This all happened in 628 AD, making Senso-ji the oldest temple in Tokyo. Even with the usual crowds and noise, the sheer size of everything is simply awe-inspiring. Inside there is a five-story pagoda, trails of incense and several temple halls to explore.
Free • 24h

Kaminarimon

3) Benten-do
A mainly unknown shrine to the east of Senso-ji. Inside, **The Bell of Time** is a cast-bronze bell that was used as an hour bell by the Tokugawa shogunate in 1692. These days, it gets hit at 6am, if you are able to get up early enough. Note that the actual shrine grounds are often closed, so check at your hotel or an information center beforehand.
Free • 11am-7pm

4) Denboin-dori Street
Shops and signs reminiscent of old Tokyo, with some almost looking like shacks. As you start to walk down here and into the other streets west of Nakamise-dori, things get more down to earth. The shops will cater more to locals, with a splattering of places to pick up things like a traditional fan or yukata.

5) Hoppy Street
Asakusa's most famous spot for drinking and eating out. It's mostly old fashioned izakayas and outdoor bars here, and while it gets crowded, the atmosphere is amazing.

Most of the restaurants here serve nikomi. An inexpensive stew made with beef tendons and mixed vegetables, each spot will have its own twist on it. Comfy favorites like yakitori and sashimi are readily available, so it's best to stroll down and head into whatever takes your fancy.

6) Asakusa Hanayashiki
Forget Disneyland, this is the real deal! Hanayashiki opened way back in 1853. It offers a truly old school, nostalgic experience. No big fancy VR/3D roller coasters here, but classics like a merry-go-round, swan rides and haunted houses. Oh, and a panda car too.
Access 1000 yen (rides from 100 yen), all access pass 2800 yen • 10am-6pm

7) Edo Taito Traditional Crafts Center
Excellent collection of traditional Japanese handicrafts. On weekends, the city's select artisans visit and give demonstrations of how the handicrafts are made, as well as organize hands-on experiences for visitors.
Free • 10am-6pm

8) Kappabashi Dougu Street
Ever seen plastic food models outside a Japanese restaurant, and want some of your own? Or want to check out the kind of kit that Japanese chefs use? Kappabashi is the place to come. It's lined with all sorts of shops dedicated to wooing enthusiasts and professionals, with shops selling knives, kitchenware, shop signs and lots more.

9) Drum Museum
Taiko drums have been making a name for themselves across the world, and this is the premier spot to see and learn about them. Opened by Miyamoto-Unosuke, a company that has been building Taiko since 1861, it has a collection of around 800 drums. Visitors can also have a play if they like.
500 yen • 10am-5pm • Closed on Mondays and Tuesdays (except national holidays)

Recommended cafe
Try fruit sandwiches at Sukemasa Coffee, as well as a brew using beans brought over from Kanagawa. There are some cool extra touches, like the macchiato served in a Japanese sake cup, and the latte served in a delicate porcelain cup.
Snacks and drinks from 500 yen • 11am-6pm • Closed on Tuesdays

Recommended meal spot
Finish your walk with an okonomiyaki (Japanese pancake) and other tasty grilled plates at Sometaro. Cooking instructions and English-speaking staff available.
From 900 yen • 12am-8:15pm • Closed on Tuesdays

Plastic food models in Kappabashi

Crossing the Rainbow Bridge – Odaiba

DISTANCE: 10 KM | BICYCLES NEED TO BE WALKED ON THE BRIDGE

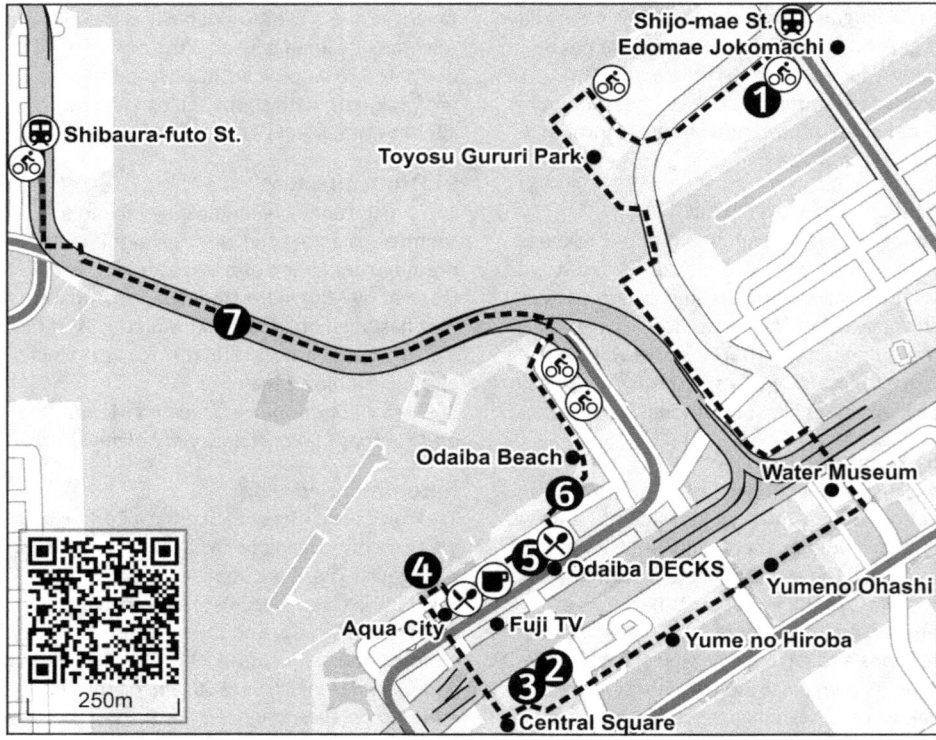

Odaiba, and the other man-made islands surrounding it on the Tokyo Bay, are go-to areas for shopping and seaside pleasures. Do this path if you want a day of modern Tokyo. Note that some areas ask cyclists to get off their bikes, but it's mostly doable by bicycle.

Starting and ending points

First, make your way to Shijo-mae Station on the Yurikamome Line, then follow signs to Toyosu Market. You'll finish the route up at Shibaura-futo, on the same line.

Places of interest

1) Toyosu Market

After replacing Tsukiji Market in 2018, Toyosu became the main market for seafood, fruits and vegetables in Tokyo. The new complex is much better set up for tourists, with viewing platforms, tourist-friendly dining and shopping areas, and the world famous tuna auctions in the early mornings.

Next door is the brand new Edomae Jokomachi, an off-market dining and shopping area with sellers that use the market's produce and fish (9am-9pm). To book a spot for the tuna auction see shijou.metro.tokyo.lg.jp/english/toyosu.
Free • 5am-3pm

2) Poop Museum Tokyo

This spot bills itself as a 'poop-orientated entertainment facility'. Via a variety of colorful kawaii unko (cute poop), the museum takes a very silly look at something only the Japanese could make a whole museum about.
1800-2300 yen • 11pm-8pm

View over Tokyo Bay, towards the Rainbow Bridge

3) Unicorn Gundam Statue
A full-scale statue of a Gundam character, a Japanese mega franchise similar to Transformers. Standing at almost 20 meters tall, it also occasionally switches modes and changes shape. A must-do selfie spot.

4) Statue of Liberty
On the north side of the main island the **Odaiba Seaside Park**, looking spick and span after its Olympic Games renewal, is a great place to chill. There's a sandy beach and views over Tokyo Bay, plus the replica of the Statue of Liberty. It may only be 11 meters high, but the view makes it another must-do.

5) Tokyo Joypolis
An indoor amusement park created by SEGA, best known for Sonic the Hedgehog. The site is crammed with more than 20 attractions, such as VR rides, laser tag, a rollercoaster and all sorts of other daredevil craziness. Discounts are available in the evening, on your birthday and on your birthday month, so check tokyo-joypolis.com before visiting.
Entry 800 yen, day pass 4500 yen • 11am-7pm (until 8pm on weekends and holidays)

6) Daiba Park
Odaiba was originally built to provide maritime defense. The area that is now Daiba Park used to be a military fort, with steep stone walls and clear views over the bay. Much of this history remains to this day, and you'll be able to see the ammunition and explosive warehouses, as well as a replica of a gun battery from the Edo period.
Free • 24h

7) Rainbow Bridge
Named so for its multicolored lights, this is Tokyo's most iconic bridge, and luckily it features walking paths on both sides.

For the best views, head over the bridge at nighttime, on the north side. This will give you spectacular night views of central Tokyo, from Tokyo Tower to the SkyTree. If the skies are particularly clear, though, you can see Mount Fuji from the south side!
9am-9pm (April to October), 10am-6pm (November to March) • Closed on the third Monday of each month (except national holidays) and in extreme weather

Recommended cafe
Back when Eggs 'n Things first opened in Harajuku in 2010, there were queues around the block. They have since expanded to spots such as Aqua City Odaiba. This Japanese take on Hawaiian cuisine has hearty all-day breakfasts, but the real draw is their signature pancakes. As well as being accompanied by what seems like a mountain of whipped cream on top, the restaurant also has inventive monthly specials.
Pancakes from 800 yen, drinks 400-800 yen • 9am-10pm

Recommended meal spot
Odaiba Takoyaki Museum is the place to come for Takoyaki fans (octopus balls). Some of Osaka's best have come together in this convenient spot in Decks Tokyo Beach. Next door, Aqua City Odaiba houses the Tokyo Ramen Kokugikan Mai, a collection of famous noodle restaurants, all in one convenient location.
Meals 800-1000 yen • 11am-8pm

View from Odaiba Beach

Shinkansen, characters and ramen – Tokyo Station area

DISTANCE: 1-2 KM | BEST ON FOOT

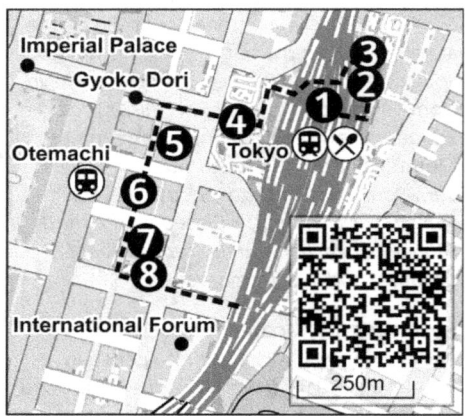

Tokyo Station is naturally one of the capital's major transportation hubs, with the accolade of being the busiest station by the number of trains. The station itself has a wide array of shopping opportunities, plus the surrounding area has really been spruced up with huge, glass-paneled skyscrapers and a collection of revived classical buildings.

Starting and ending points

For this walk it'll be better to come on a JR line, such as the Yamanote Line, but the Tokyo Metro Marunouchi Line also reaches Tokyo. The route begins on the station's ground floor, from which you need to head east for the Yaesu side. You'll eventually finish back at the station.

Places of interest

1) GRANSTA
The newest, and possibly largest, in-station shopping and dining spot. Split into two areas, GRANSTA is located on the ground and B1 floors. Inside are a labyrinth of gift shops, posh bakeries, boutique fashion shops and casual meal options. There are also 'ekiben', bento boxes unique to the station, that Japanese visitors to Tokyo love to enjoy on their return home. It's all located in the JR ticket area, but if you are entering from outside you can purchase a general admission ticket from a JR vending machine (140 yen).
8pm-10pm (until 9pm on weekends)

2) Tokyo Character Street
Come out of the JR ticket area via the Yaesu Central Exit and head to **First Avenue** for this insanely popular collection of character stores. You're spoilt for choice if you want to pick up some cute gifts or clothes, with about two dozen stores from the likes of Pokemon, One Piece and Hello Kitty and Rilakkuma. It can seem a little overwhelming inside, so give yourself plenty of time to soak it in.
10am-10pm

3) Tokyo Okashi Land
Near Tokyo Character Street is this sweetie paradise. All the major Japanese candy and chocolate makers are here, as well as Kyoro-chan, the adorable mascot of Morinaga Milk. Limited edition snacks and pop-up stores from smaller producers are also available..

Many stores have a demonstration kitchen, where you can get freshly-made sweets. For example, at the **Calbee** store customers can choose from a menu of toppings and flavors for their potato chips, then see them deep-fried there and then.
9am-9pm

Tokyo Station

Relaxing at Naka-Dori

4) Marunouchi Ekimae Square
Check out the red-brick façade of the wonderfully restored station's west side. From here continue down **Gyoko-dori**, a pedestrian area heading towards the **Imperial Palace**. The contrast between the grand skyscrapers to your sides, the magnificent station behind you and the palace ahead will make for a truly memorable moment!

5) Marunouchi Building
The original Marunouchi Building was built in 1923 and became famous for surviving the Great Kanto Earthquake. In more modern times though, this newer 37-story skyscraper was built by Japanese conglomerate Mitsubishi Group to house their offices. The lower levels contain upmarket shops and restaurants, with an inside meant to recreate the appearance of the original building. Head to the 35th floor for views over Tokyo Station.

6) Naka-Dori Avenue
This charming tree-lined road is the main shopping street in Marunouchi. It has a slightly European feel, with cafes that have set up outdoor tables and food trucks parking up for lunchtime. In wintertime the trees are wrapped in more than a million LED lights.

7) Marunouchi Brick Square
Take a breather at this little oasis. Brick Square is described as a European-style courtyard and square, nestled between all the modern office buildings. Relax your feet from all the walking in front of the fountain, flowers and modern sculptures.
11am-11pm

8) Mitsubishi Ichigokan Museum
Next door to the Brick Square is this extraordinary museum (reopening autumn 2024). Housed in a recreation of a 1894 Western-style office building, the museum features a collection of paintings by Toulouse-Lautrec, Odilon Redon and Félix Vallotton. The special exhibitions, which also tend to focus on traditional Western art, usually cover late 19th century to early 20th century art. Excellent English explanations provided.
1000 yen • 9am-5pm

Recommended cafe
Avoid the expensive cafes here and head to Bake Cheese Tart in GRANSTA. Made on site, the seasonal cheese tarts, with flavors like strawberry and matcha, are always popular.
Tarts 230-300 yen • 8am-10pm

Recommended meal spot
Bringing together some of the best ramen restaurants in the city, Tokyo Ramen Street in First Avenue (B1 floor) should have something for everyone. Each restaurant has its own unique dish, mastered to perfection, from classics like tonkotsu to more original creations. My top choice is **Tsujita Miso no Sho**, which uses several types of miso to create an incredibly rich broth.
Bowls around 750-1000 yen • 10:30am-11pm

Combine with...
The Imperial Palace walk starts a few minutes west of this one, so it would be an easy way to expand your walk to a day-long one.

The view towards the Imperial Palace

Shinjuku's skyscraper district – Nishi-Shinjuku

DISTANCE: 3.5 KM | POSSIBLE ON BICYCLE OR FOOT

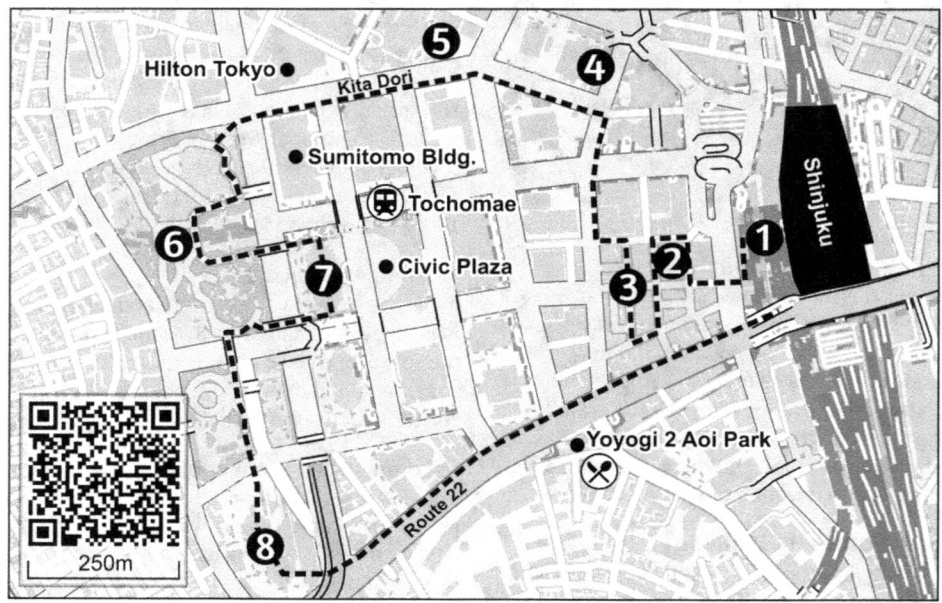

To the west side of Shinjuku Station is the skyscraper district of Nishi-Shinjuku. This area was in fact the city's first designated zone for skyscrapers, which appeared during the 1970s boom period. As well as the HQs of various big companies, the Tokyo Metropolitan Government is located here.

Starting and ending points

Shinjuku station is on a bunch of lines, such as the JR Yamanote, Toei Oedo Line and the Tokyo Metro Marunouchi Line. Make your way to the west side and follow directions to the Keio Department Store, on the south west side. Cross the main road to begin.

The route finishes back at Shinjuku Station. If you don't want to venture up for a drink at the Park Hyatt at the end, you could alternatively come back via Tochomae Station (connected to the Tokyo Metropolitan Government Building).

Places of interest

1) Keio Department Store

Owned by one of the other train companies that heads into Shinjuku, Keio, this 'departo' is one of the major shopping complexes in the web of buildings surrounding the station. It's considered to be more for budget-conscious consumers than rivals like Takashimaya, and has frequent sales. Pop up to the sixth floor to see some traditional Japanese crafts, calligraphy tools and Daruma dolls.
10am-8:30pm (until 8pm on Sundays)

2) Yodobashi Camera

This nationwide electronics chain has an array of specialist stores scattered around this shopping and drinking district. As well as a camera store, there are also ones for toys and hobbies, watches, games and accessories.
9:30am-10pm

Electronics stores on Shinjuku's west side

3) Chuo-dori, Nibandai and Sanbangai Streets
Around the area with all the Yodobashi Cameras are more izakayas (Japanese bars) than anyone could ever need. During the daytime you'll find a few discount lunch menus, but be sure to return in the evening to enjoy the more boisterous atmosphere that night and plenty of alcohol brings! Many of the restaurants cater to foreign tourists with multilingual menus and staff.

4) Sompo Museum of Art
Six-story museum holding exhibitions of Japanese and foreign artists. In its collection is a version of Van Gogh's Sunflowers, with temporary exhibitions changing frequently throughout the year. Visit sompo-museum.org to see what's on.
1600 yen • 10am-6pm • Closed on Mondays (except national holidays)

5) LOVE sculpture
Reproduction of Robert Indiana's iconic LOVE sculpture in Philadelphia, USA. It's become an essential selfie spot. There are a few other sculptures outside the Shinjuku i-land building to keep an eye out for, too, as you walk ahead.

6) Shinjuku Central Park
This is the place where all the business people and bureaucrats come for a bento lunch, and presumably for a bit of an escape from work. On the weekends flea markets are often held, but it's generally a very peaceful spot on weekdays.
Free • 24h

7) Tokyo Metropolitan Building
While not as high as the SkyTree, the observation decks at the top of this building provide commanding views over the capital, and for free. On clear days you'll be able to see Mount Fuji to the west, and Odaiba to the east. If open, the south observatory is more fully featured, with a cafe, souvenir shop and an open piano.
Free • 9:30am-10pm

8) Park Hyatt Tokyo
If you're a movie fan, the **New York Bar** up the Park Hyatt is unmissable, though for any city slicker it's also an amazing experience. This is the place western celebrities usually come to stay in Tokyo, and was heavily featured in the Hollywood movie Lost in Translation, starring Bill Murray and Scarlett Johansson. There is a dress code, but as long as you don't enter with a sleeveless top and shorts you should be fine.
Drinks from 1300 yen (+ cover charges from 8pm on most nights) • 5pm-11pm (Sundays to Wednesdays), 5pm-12am (Thursdays to Saturdays

Recommended meal spot
Local joint Fuunji is famous for its tsukemen (dipping noodles). Served with a thick broth, it's recommended to get the deluxe set which comes with big chunks of pork, an egg and bamboo shoots. Don't let any potential line put you off, it'll be well worth it.
Tsukemen 900-1100 yen • 11am-2pm, 5:30pm-9pm

Shinjuku at night

Exploring Tokyo's Korea Town – Shin-Okubo

DISTANCE: 2 KM | BEST ON FOOT

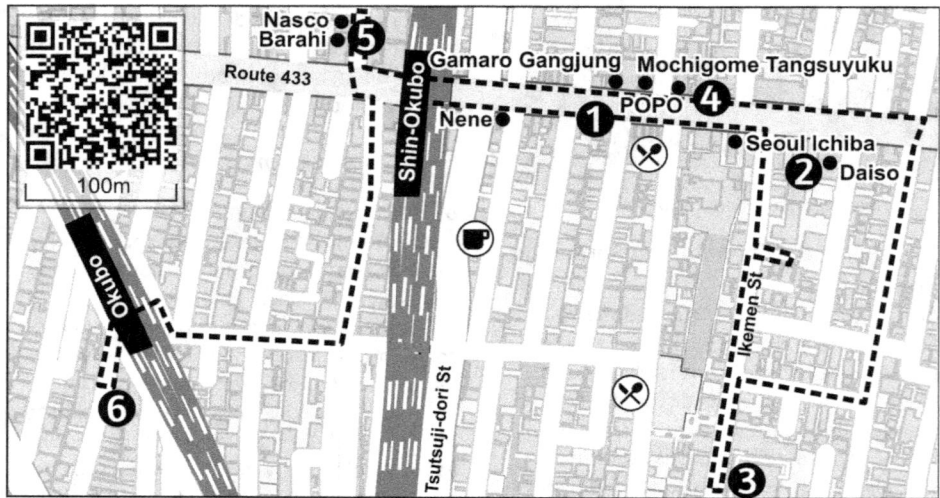

Sometimes known as K-Town, the Shin-Okubo area is the place to see how the cute and crazy aspects of these two countries combine. It's full of idol shops selling posters, CDs and DVDs of the latest stars, as well as the heartthrobs of the past. It attracts both the young and old, who come here to immerse themselves in Korean culture, fashion and cosmetics. It's not all about Korea though, as you'll discover on this walk.

Starting and ending points

Make your way to Shin-Okubo Station (Main Exit), which is one stop from Shinjuku on the JR Yamanote Line. Take a right and walk down the main road to begin. The route then ends at Shin-Okubo Station (South Entrance), also one stop from Shinjuku, on the JR Sobu Line.

Places of interest

1) Main Street (South Side)
The first Korean highlight today is **Nene Chicken** (10:30am-12am), which specializes in Korean deep-fried chicken. They can get pretty spicy, but there are various sauces which you can add and experiment with.

Shortly before you make a turn into the side streets is **Seoul Ichiba** (9am-11pm). One of the several Korean supermarkets on the road, this one is popular with Korean expats due to the reasonable prices. Also has stalls selling Korean cakes and confectionery, plus freshly made snacks to indulge in.

2) Mannenyu
Traditional public bath house, hidden down a side street beside a Daiso 100-yen store. It's got all the essentials, including a jet stream bath, an extra hot bath and a cold bath. There is also an electric bath, which has a weak electric current running through it, providing rather strange sensations!
500 yen • 3pm-12am

An example of an idol shop in Shin-Okubo

3) Don Quijote

If you don't already know, Don Quijote is a megastore chain in Japan, full to the brim with a mind-boggling variety of items. As this branch is in Korea Town, it also has plenty of Korean products, and often at better prices than elsewhere. It's a noisy, exciting experience inside, and anyone coming to Japan has got to visit at least one 'Donki'.
24h

4) Main Street (North Side)

There are loads more Korean snack and takeaway joints on this side, plus a few more idol shops. You'll soon come across the crowds outside of **POPO Hotteok** (10am-8pm). Hotteok is a sweet Korean pancake that is a popular street food in South Korea. POPO caters well to Japanese tastes, with Japanese red bean, cheese and chocolate fillings, as well as Korean classics like kimchi.

A little further down **Chicken Mochigome Tangsuyuku** (9am-9pm) sells delicious Korean oden (stewed fishcakes, eggs and vegetables) and **Gamaro Gangjung** (9am-8pm) offers Korean battered hot dogs, smothered in cheese and spicy sauce. Rainbow-colored cheese inside the hot dog is also an option!

5) Islam Alley

As well as the Korean, Taiwanese and Chinese people that have made Shin-Okubo their home, in recent years the number of people coming from India, Pakistan and the Middle East has increased significantly. This side street, dubbed by locals as Islam Alley, is lined with halal grocery stores and restaurants, and feels at points a world away from Japan.

Favorites along the way include **Green Nasco** (10am-11pm), a highly rated grocery store, with a food court next door that serves killer barbecued chicken and biryani. Also be sure to check out **Barahi Foods & Spice Center** (10am-11pm), which is great for Indian and Nepalese cooking. There is a restaurant on the second floor where you can try authentic Nepalese cuisine, rather than the ones heavily adapted for Japanese tastes.
Free • 6am-5pm

A typical afternoon in Shin-Okubo

6) Tokyo Mazu Temple

A beautiful Chinese temple dedicated to the sea goddess Mazu. It really stands out in this back alley, with its vibrant red and gold pillars and Chinese wall paintings. A large number of Taiwanese people also live in the area, and it only opened in 2013. It's a rather different looking, if welcome, addition to the area.
Free • 9am-5:30pm (until 2pm on Fridays)

Recommended cafe

You might have to do a double take when you first look into 2D Cafe. For a second the interior looks like a flat, 2D illustration. The walls and furniture look like they have been taken out of a black and white manga comic, and even the window curtains and flowers are paintings rather than the real thing. 2D Cafe has a wide selection of bubble teas and shaved ice desserts, but the main reason to come here is to get those sweet Instagram pics.
From 1000 per person • 11am-10pm

Recommended meal spots

As you walk around you'll be inundated with meal options. One favorite of local Koreans is Samgyeopsal, a kind of Korean pork belly barbeque. At most restaurants the meat is grilled in front of you by the staff. The meat is then wrapped up in lettuce, then spicy sauces and kimchi can be added. Well known ones include **Nangman_29** (11am-11pm) and **Macchan** (11am-11pm), but keep a lookout for current deals on offer as you do the walk.
Usually from around 1000 per person

Tokyo's central Olympic area – Shinjuku to Akasaka

DISTANCE: 6.5 KM | BEST IN AUTUMN, BUT GREAT IN ANY SEASON

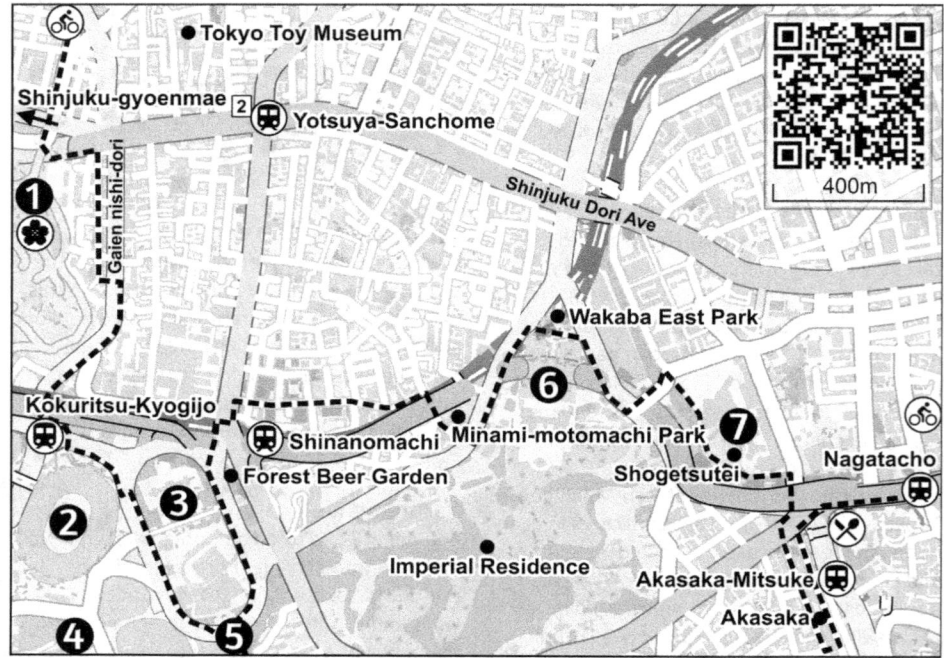

While it's usually quite difficult to cycle in the city center, due to all the crowds and lack of cycling lanes, this chapter is a neat route via mostly wide, quiet roads. It'll zigzag you through palace grounds, gardens and some non-touristy neighborhoods. There just might be a few spots where you'll have to get off your bicycle. It's also doable as a long walk, if you are so inclined.

Starting and ending points

Get started at Shinjuku-Gyoen Station (Exit 2), which is on the Tokyo Metro Marunouchi Line. There are bicycle stations a short walk away. You'll eventually end up near Nagatacho Station, also on the Tokyo Metro.

Places of interest

1) Shinjuku Gyoen National Garden

Formerly the private mansion and grounds of a feudal lord in the Edo era, Shinjuku Gyoen is now a beloved nature hotspot for workers and residents of Shinjuku. Covering over 144 acres, it's helpfully split up into sections. There's an English garden, a Japanese garden, a landscape garden, the list goes on! Give yourself at least an hour to enjoy it all.
500 yen • 9am-5:30pm • Closed on Mondays (except national holidays)

2) Japan National Stadium

A colossal sports arena, and the centerpiece of Tokyo's Olympic and Paralympic events. This isn't your usual stadium though, as it's surrounded by a wooden lattice framework that uses Ryukyu Pine and cedarwood from each of Japan's 47 prefectures. It's the perfect combination of modern and traditional Japanese architecture.

It's now possible to visit the stadium. The tour takes visitors inside, seeing where the athletes spent their time before and after events, plus there are opportunities to get a photo on the Olympic podium and an

amusing video of yourself jumping over a hurdle.
Tour 1800 yen • 10am-6pm (check kokuritu-tours.jp for operating days)

State Guest House

3) Meiji Memorial Museum
A collection of great works from the most influential artists of the Meiji era (1868-1912). The approximately 80 pieces offer an excellent insight into the history, politics and culture of the period. Along the way, chronologically displayed murals retell the major events that took place, from the birth to the demise of the Meiji emperor.
500 yen • 9am-5pm

4) Japan Olympic Museum
Most people never got a chance to be in Japan during its Olympics, but the official museum makes a great effort to tell Japan's Olympic journey, right back to its first participation in 1912.

Inside, the Exhibition Area has a bunch of hands-on experiences, such as simulators for shooting and ski jumping, while the Monument Area shows off various medals and statues. There are also displays of relay torches, sports equipment and the like.
500 yen • 10am-5pm • Closed on Mondays (except national holidays)

5) Jingu Gaien Ginkgo Avenue
146 ginkgo trees, each precisely planted 9 meters apart, running down a grand avenue. It's rather unique in its scale, and an essential visit during autumn.

6) State Guest House Akasaka Palace
When royalty or dignitaries from across the world visit Japan, this is where they get to stay. The guest house is a neo-baroque building with elaborate receptions and dining rooms that resemble a British palace, something quite unique in Tokyo. You should definitely stop off along the route for a photo.

Even better, if you can, is to head inside. You'll be able to enter the main building and gardens by signing in at reception on the day, but reservations offer the chance to enter the Japanese-style annex too. Book via geihinkan.go.jp/Akasaka.
Free • 6am-5pm

7) Hotel New Otani Japanese Garden
Consistently ranked as one of the best free attractions in Japan, this super posh hotel's garden used to be the property of a variety of samurai. The grounds feature ancient stone lanterns, koi and carp ponds and a stone garden, plus is reasonably well known for its seasonal flowers and foliage. A classic Japanese garden experience for sure.
Free • 9am-10pm

The Japanese garden at Hotel New Otani

Recommended cafe
Royal Garden Cafe Aoyama offers splendid views towards the ginkgo trees from its outdoor terrace. It's a very classy cafe, with a small but lovingly designed menu of home-baked breads and cakes, plus light pasta and pizza meals.
Cakes and snacks from 800 yen, drinks 550-1200 yen • 11am-10pm

Recommended meal spot
Dine with the ninjas at Ninja Tokyo. It's hidden deep inside a ninja hideout, so watch out for the genuinely high quality Japanese food, magic tricks and ninja attacks.
Meals 880-2585 yen • 11am-11pm

The gateway to Hibiya Park – Minato City
DISTANCE: 5 KM | BEST ON FOOT, BUT POSSIBLE ON BICYCLE

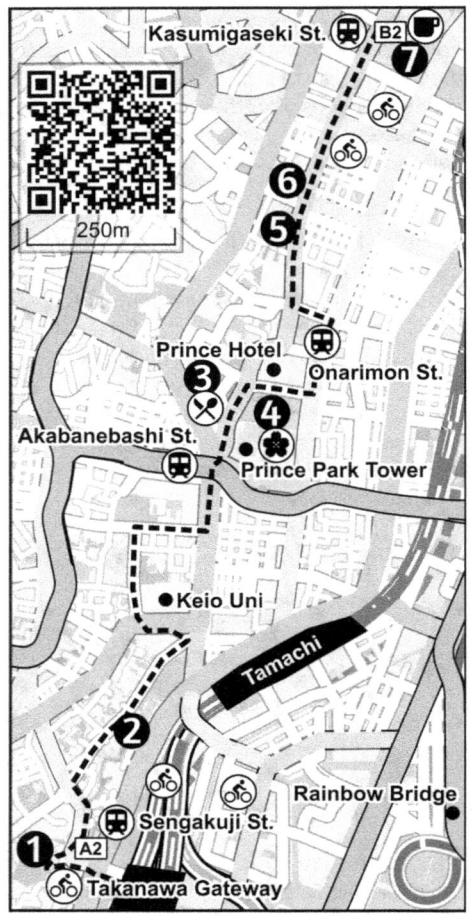

Starting and ending points

Make your way on the Yamanote or Keihin-Tohoku lines to Takanawa Gateway, then take the West Exit. Alternatively, you could start from Sengakuji Station (Exit 2A) on the Asakusa Line of the Toei Subway.

From either station follow signs west to Sengakuji Temple, the first stop. The walk ends at Kasumigaseki Station (Exit B2), at the west entrance of Hibiya Park, which is on the Tokyo Metro Chiyoda, Hibiya and Marunouchi lines.

Places of interest

1) Sengakuji Temple

Although it's one of the most famous Buddhist temples in Japan, Sengakuji is a surprisingly quiet spot on most days. First constructed by Tokugawa Ieyasu in 1612, a Shogun during the Edo era, it has since had a long and rich history.

The most well-known story is the one of the 47 Ronin, also known as the Ako Incident. After their feudal lord was compelled to commit 'seppuku' (ritual suicide) for attacking a court official by the name of Kira Yoshinaka, a now leaderless 47 samurai took revenge by killing Kira. Unfortunately, they then had to perform seppuku on themselves, for committing the crime of murder. The story has since become a legend known across Japan.

As well as learning about the temple's history, exploring the well-maintained Buddhist temples grounds will reveal some interesting statues and Buddhist structures, as well as a Buddhist graveyard.
Free • 7am-6pm (until 5pm October to March)

2) Mita Hachiman Jinja

Said to have been established all the way back in 709, this shrine was built to enshrine the guardian deity of Japan's eastern

Takanawa Okido, around what is now Sengakuji Station, used to be known as a gateway to Edo, the old name for Tokyo. This route therefore appropriately starts at Takanawa Gateway Station. Settlements based around temples and shrines were formed along the major route north to Mita up on the northern end, with the most prominent being Zojoji. Towards the end of the Tokugawa shogunate many of the temples were used as foreign diplomatic establishments, and to this day a large number of embassies are based in this area.

provinces. It became a center of worship for the local Watanabe clan, and now houses some of the oldest 'koma-inu' stone dog statues in Kanto.
Free • 9am-5pm

3) Tokyo Tower
The older brother of the now more famous Tokyo SkyTree, Tokyo Tower was built in 1958 as a symbol of Japan's rebirth after WW2. Standing at 333 meters, the observation deck still provides amazing views over the capital. A modern VR and amusement area has also been built on the bottom floor.
Adults from 1200 yen, children from 500-1000 yen • 9am-10:30pm

4) Zojoji
With its main gate imposingly standing out along this main road, this temple is hard to miss. An impressive complex awaits visitors inside, one that has been depicted in artistic works throughout the generations, particularly ukiyo-e prints by Utagawa Hiroshige. There is also a garden with rows of small 'Jizo' stone statues.

The downstairs Zojoji Treasures Gallery contains a spectacular 1:10 scale model of the Taitokuin Mausoleum, a vast complex that used to surround Zojoji. Destroyed in bombing raids, its magnificent decorations and elaborate architecture are thought to be the inspirations for Toshogu Shrine in Nikko, a World Heritage Site.
FREE (Treasure Gallery 700 yen) • 9am-5pm (Treasure Gallery 10am-4pm) • Closed on Tuesdays (except national holidays)

5) Stairway of Success
You'll need to push yourself to reach rustic Atago Shrine, with visitors required to climb up a steep flight of 86 stairs to complete this challenge. The ritual started after a young samurai dared to ride his horse up the hill and take several branches from the blooming plum trees at the top. After offering them to the Shogun to show how much of a skilled rider he was, he was said to have won the Shogun's admiration.

6) Toranomon Hills
A huge business, shopping and dining complex, with the main tower being the tallest building in Tokyo at a height of 255.5 meters. Be sure to check out Toranomon Yokocho, a collection of 26 posh, yet casual, restaurants and bars. Each is designed so that customers can see the chefs at work, and to create a social atmosphere reminiscent of shopping districts of the past.
24h (Yokocho 11am-11pm)

7) Hibiya Park
Japan's first Western-style park is a welcome oasis away from the hectic business districts nearby to the park. There are also some Japanese garden elements dotted around too, plus plenty of spots to relax and have a drink after your walk.
Free • 24h

Recommended cafe
Tully's Coffee, inside Hibiya Park, has a pleasant veranda from where you can relax and chill with a coffee or tea.
Drinks 750-1100 yen • 8am-7pm

Recommended meal spot
Mos Burger, a famous burger chain in Japan, sells the special 'Tower Burger' at their Tokyo Tower branch. It contains several patties, so it's another demanding challenge!
Meals 750-1100 yen • 11am-7pm

Looking up at Tokyo Tower from Zojoji

Tokyo's stylish catwalk – Daikanyama
DISTANCE: 2.5 KM | BEST ON MONDAY, WEDNESDAY OR FRIDAY

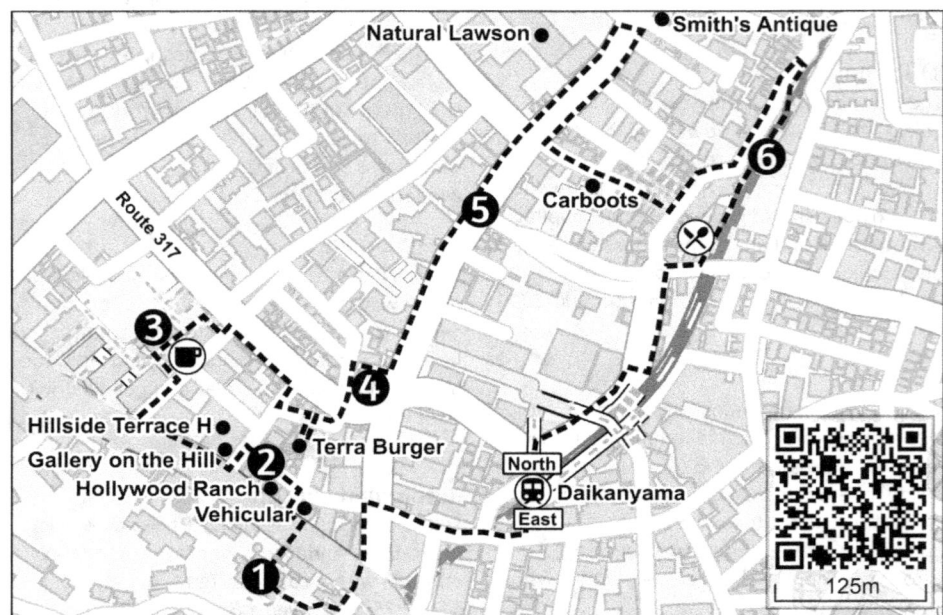

Daikanyama is known by Tokyoites as a district with a chilled vibe, home to a wide selection of trendy boutiques. It's usually a pretty quiet spot, even though it's such a short distance from the sometimes bewilderingly crowded Shibuya Station. Come here for an afternoon of peaceful window shopping, or to indulge yourself in the culinary delights on offer!

Starting and ending points

This route starts at the East Exit, and ends up at the Northern Entrance of Daikanyama Station. This is on the Tokyu Toyoko Line, and is one stop from Shibuya Station.

Places of interest

1) Kyu Asakura House

A lovely Taisho Period mansion built in 1919 by Torajiro Asakura, the former head of the Tokyo City Assembly and a wealthy landowner. Inside it's all tatami mats, delicate wooden floor boards and immaculate clapboard walls, so visitors need to remove their shoes before entering.
100 yen • 10am-6pm • Closed on Mondays (except national holidays)

2) Sarugakucho area

Let's head in and out of the backstreets of Daikanyama. There are a bunch of cool stores selling designer jeans and hipster coffee shops as you head out the station into Sarugakucho, as well as the flagship store of **Vermicular** around the corner (9am-6pm). This company sells super high-quality cast iron cookware, showing off some superb Japanese craftsmanship.

At the end of the street is **Hillside Terrace** (10am-7pm, closed weekends), a shopping mall known for organic foods, and **Gallery on the Hill**, an exhibition area that focuses on avant-garde contemporary artists, with exhibits only running for a few weeks each. **Hollywood Ranch Market** (11am-7pm) also comes highly recommended for vintage clothing.

Outside the T-Site

3) T-Site
Billing itself as a 'Library in the Woods', T-Site is a bookstore paradise run by Tsutaya, a national book rental chain. The building has won several awards not just for its Klein Dytham designed architecture, but also for what's inside its actual store.

Tsutaya Books Daikanyama houses a wide selection that's unrivaled in Tokyo, from vintage books to periodicals from around the world. Those looking for more can enter the **Anjin Library**, which has thousands of nostalgic magazines from the 60s and 70s, including Vogue and Japanese classics like Heibon Punch. After this, the stationary section is a perfect spot to get some stylish gifts for back home.
9am-10pm

4) Kamawanu
This cute little shop sells tenugui, which are traditional hand-printed cotton cloths. They can be used as gift wraps, hand towels, place mats and whatever you can imagine. Designs can be traditional as well as comical and modern, so it's a really interesting shop to venture into.
11am-7pm • Closed on Tuesdays

5) Hachiman-dori Street
Continue up this main road, which thankfully has a few convenience stores if your wallet is hurting, then head back into the backstreets for **Carboots** (12am-7pm, closed Thursdays). High quality vintage goods are all the rage here, from the likes of brands such as Celine and Hermes. There are also plenty of novelty items and random bric-a-brac to seek out.

6) Log Road Daikanyama
Keep an eye out for the shops along here, as some of Tokyo's newest and trendiest are hidden down this narrow path. Built on top of the old Tokyu Toyoko Line tracks, it's now a cluster of shops and eateries in modern wooden cottages, with regularly changing outdoor pop-up shops too.

Recommended cafe
Check out Princi in the T-Site area, an upmarket Italian bakery that now operates at many Starbucks Reserve roasteries across Japan. Classic pastries, cakes and desserts are on full display as you enter, but Princi also has Italian cocktails and exclusives like the 'Bigniolata al Cioccolato', a decadent cream puff pastry covered in a chocolate sauce.
Drinks 1200-1500 yen • 7am-8pm

Recommended meal spot
Offering a range of craft beers that are brewed on site, Spring Valley Brewery Tokyo is a microbrewery owned by the national chain Kirin. Set in a renovated warehouse, it offers honest grub such as pizzas and tapas to accompany the drinks. The menu helpfully shows which beer goes best with which dish.
Drinks from 790 yen, food 1000-2000 yen • 11am-11pm (until 10pm on Sundays)

Combine with...
Shibuya (p10) is only one station away, so you would easily expand on this course by walking to/from here, which would add about half an hour. Just head north-east and follow the Yamanote Line tracks northwards.

The entrance to Log Road Daikanyama

Checking out Tokyo's cool canals – Shinagawa
DISTANCE: 3 KM | EASIEST ON FOOT

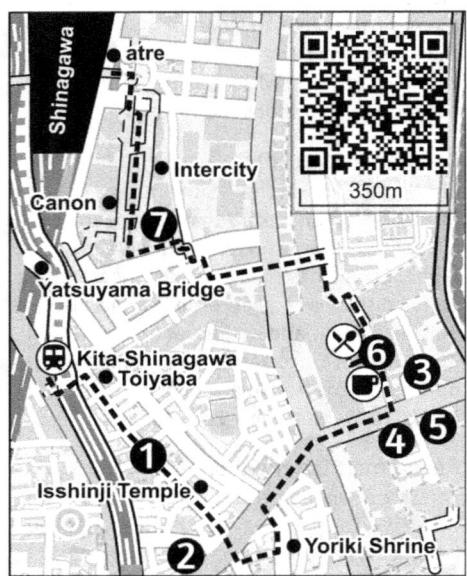

Shinagawa is one of Tokyo's main transportation hubs, being on the Shinkansen network and soon to be the Tokyo terminus of the maglev train to Kansai. Venturing a little south to Kita-Shinagawa is a classic Tokyo walk, with a mix of traditional shopping on the west side, and a modern, hip area around the canal on the east side.

Starting and ending points

The route begins at Kita-Shinagawa Station, one stop from Shinagawa on the Keikyu Line. Take a left from the exit, and head over the tracks to start your adventures. You'll end up back at Shinagawa, which is conveniently located on the JR Yamanote Line.

Places of interest

1) Kita-Shinagawa Shopping Street
Previously a port station in the Edo era. There are still plenty of wooden-built stores that look like they are from that period, but the real charm of this place is the local life. It's a quiet shopping street, mostly devoid of chains, where everyday people go about their business. The mom-and-pop greengrocers, butchers and toy shops, plus some no-fuss Japanese restaurants, provide a nice glimpse into everyday Tokyo life. Head into the TOIYABA Tourist Information Center to find out more about the area.

2) Kitashinagawa Spa Tenjinyu
A modern sento (public baths) that feels more upmarket than most, Tenjinyu is known for its black amber colored water. This color comes from all the fallen plants that permeated the groundwater millions of years ago in the area, meaning it is silky smooth and rich in minerals.

Tenjinyu caters well to foreign tourists that don't know all the rules and etiquette, with clear English explanations and signage. The almost pitch black water also helps if you are a little shy!
500 yen • 3pm-11pm

3) Tennozu Isle
This artificial island has transformed many of its once presumably dank industrial warehouses into a hip canal-side neighborhood. It's the perfect spot for a summer stroll, with plenty of spots to sit down at and chill. Below are some highlights.

Chilling out along the canals

4) WHAT Museum
A warehouse museum that focuses on making private collections available to the public, as

well as showing off up-and-coming artists. Alongside the exhibits the collectors and artists have shared their thoughts on the works they own or created, offering a deeper insight into the art and sculptures.
1200 yen • 11am-7pm • Closed on Mondays (except national holidays)

5) Pigment
Designed by world-renowned artist Kengo Kuma, this unique store specializes in rare painting utensils, and has a bewildering display of art materials and paints. The building has a dynamic, modern bamboo themed interior, with a display of more than 4,500 colors, interesting workshops and lots of cutting-edge technologies to check out.
11am-7pm • Closed on Mondays (except national holidays)

Looking towards Bond Street

6) Bond Street
Unfortunately not related to 007, here Bond refers to how the area used to hold imported goods that were inspected for tax duties. Nowadays the street is lined with vibrant murals and graffiti spanning multi-story buildings, something that is certainly an unexpected sight in Tokyo.

7) Nikon Museum
Housed on the east side of **Shinagawa Intercity**, a vast business complex with a garden running through it, the Nikon Museum exhibits the history, products and latest technologies of one of the world's oldest and largest camera companies. Inside you'll also see how cameras are used in space exploration and the work of David Douglas Duncan, who made the brand famous across the world with his photography during the Korean War, as well as his photos of Picasso. Canon also has a showroom and gallery on the other side of **Shinagawa Intercity**, which is worth a visit if you have some time left.
Free • 10am-5pm

8) atré Shinagawa
A small shopping mall located on the east side of Shinagawa Station. First to try is Dean & Deluca, which has a huge range of bakery items on the second floor. Up on the third floor there are a bunch of premium brands, such as the Isetan Queen supermarket and food court with Miyazaki style chicken. There are also a bunch of window shopping and Japanese snacking opportunities inside the JR ticket gates too.
7am-11pm

Recommended cafe
WHAT Cafe has got to be the most spacious cafe in Tokyo. Surrounded by the gallery's art, visitors can grab a barista-made coffee, craft beer, or alternatively a light meal.
Drinks 450-800 yen • 11am-6pm

Recommended meal spot
T.Y. Harbor is an American restaurant offering a decent selection of craft beers and a modern cuisine. The meals are prepared by an American chef, and include classics like sub sandwiches, burgers and grilled steaks.
Meals 1000-2000 yen at lunch, 1000-4000 yen at dinner • 11:30am-11pm

Looking down at the harbour

Transit time adventures – Haneda Airport
DISTANCE: 6 KM | BEST BY BICYCLE BUT WALKABLE

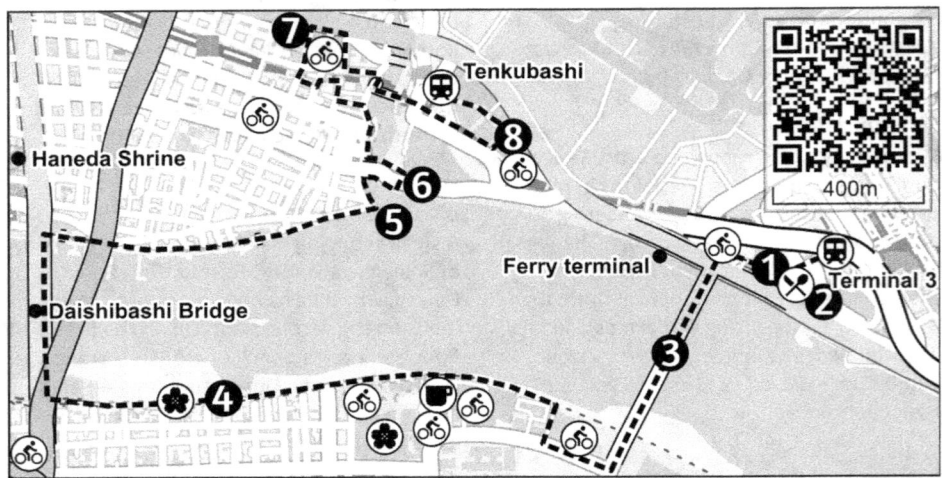

This is a perfect route to do if you have a few hours to kill before a flight, or are a bit of a plane spotter. As well as some exciting new developments on both sides of Tama River, there are still elements of a rough and ready neighborhood in the Haneda district.

Starting and ending points

First head to Haneda Terminal 3, then to Airport Garden. Outside there are bicycles from HelloCycling and Docomo, or if you want you could just walk this course. It then finishes at Tenkubashi Station, which also has some bicycle stations nearby, but you could also continue east, back to Airport Garden, if you want to use its hot spring at the end.

Places of interest

1) Airport Garden
The newest development at Haneda, directly connected to the airport via the **Japan Promenade**, an indoor Japanese 'street' lined with both traditional and modern goods and foods from across the country. Airport Garden then itself has **Haneda Sando**, full of more 'made in Japan' products. There is also a food court and tax-free shops selling travel and high-end fashion items.
8pm-11pm

2) Spa Izumi
This has got to be the height of luxury when it comes to hot springs. On the top of the Hotel Villa Fontaine, Spa Izumi uses natural hot spring water and has panoramic views over Haneda, allowing you to soak your body as you watch planes coming and going. You can also pamper yourself with massages and Korean body scrubs as optional extras. Towels and gown included.
4800 yen • 24h (baths closed 10am-1pm)

Haneda's indoor shopping streets

The Former Anamori Inari Shrine Gate

3) Tamagawa Sky Bridge
Built in tandem with Airport Garden, this bridge provides a convenient way to cross Tama River from the airport. Separate lanes for bicycles are very welcome, as are views of the city and Mount Fuji to the west, and the mouth of Tama River to the east.

4) Tama River Cycling Road
Both sides of the Tama River are very accessible for cyclists, and walkers, with mostly flat, dedicated paths along the way. If you are keen to see more of the river, it's perfectly possible to continue up as far as you like and return via the other side when ready.

5) Gojukkenbana Muenbotoke Pagoda
Not much is known about the origins of this miniature Buddhist temple, located on a tiny concrete island out into Tama River. Said to be a temple for enshrining those who lost their lives in the sea nearby, originally a square pagoda stood here. Nowadays it's kept in shape by local fishery associations and is accessible via a ramshackle bridge.
Free • 24h

6) Former Anamori Inari Shrine Gate
The below Anamori Inari Shrine used to be located on what is now the site of Haneda Airport. The shrine became popular in the late 19th century when hot springs were discovered in front of it, but when Haneda was expanded following World War II it needed to be moved. Its red gate, which usually stand at the front of Shinto shrines, remained for some time though.

Legend has it that when workers attempted to move it the thick rope snapped off, injuring a worker, who soon died of an unknown illness. Believing it to be a curse, its removal was eventually canceled. It was eventually moved to its current location when Haneda expanded in the 1990s, even if the curse did bring heavy rain.
Free • 24h

7) Anamori Inari Shrine
Next you can see the relocated shrine, founded in 1804 but which has been located in the new site since 1945. There's a good amount to see here apart from the corridor of red torii gates, such as a rooftop shrine and an indoor one filled with hundreds of model torii gates and worshipers.
Free • 8:30am-5pm

8) Footbath Skydeck
On the rooftop of the **Haneda Innovation City** building is this unique footbath. Overlooking Haneda Airport, it offers a superb viewpoint from which to take photos of the planes. Chilling out here is the perfect reward after your walk or bike ride. Towels are available from vending machines for 500 yen.
Free • 5:30am-23:30pm

Recommended cafe
Trex Kawasaki River Cafe is a cozy river spot on the south side of Tama River, with what it calls a NY French style of menu. It's become quite a favorite for cyclists and walkers on the river, with many speaking highly of the pizzas.
Drinks from 500 yen, lunches from 1300 yen • 11am-9pm (from 9am on weekends)

Recommended meal spot
Japan Loves Curry, run by the Go Go Curry chain of Japanese restaurants, will be perfect if you've just come off a flight and need a big meal. The Japanese curry is thick and strong tasting, and comes with unlimited cabbage refills. Indian curry is also available, as well as some funny face shaped curries for the kids.
Meals around 800-1200 yen • 11am-9pm

Taking the Sumida River to the Skytree – Oji to Oshiage

DISTANCE: 14 KM | BEST ON BICYCLE

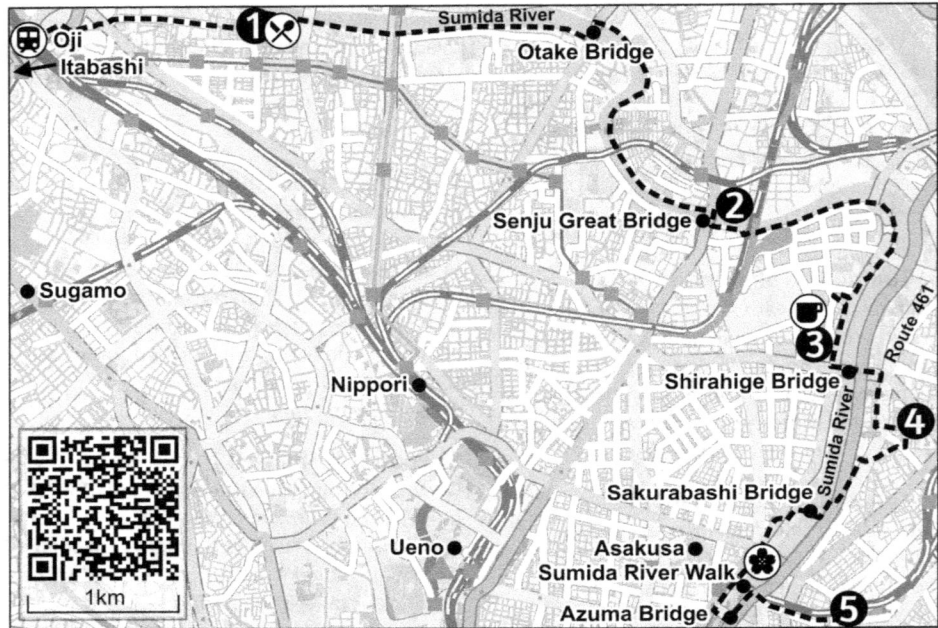

Sumida River flows through some of east Tokyo's favorite spots, such as Asakusa, Ryogoku and of course the Skytree area. Locals will often take a stroll or cycle ride on it, reveling in the cool air, pleasant vistas and simple waterside parks along the way.

While it would be perfectly possible just to take a stroll along the river near the Skytree, if you have a day free then cycling from further north is a neat idea.

Starting and ending points

First make your way to Oji, on the JR Keihin-Tohoku and Tokyo Subway Namboku lines. Pick up a bicycle from the east side of the station. You'll then finish at the Skytree, which has a bunch of lines to take you back.

Places of interest

1) Arakawa Amusement Park

Mainly child-friendly amusements, so drop off here if you're cycling with kids. As well as train and water rides, there's a small zoo with ponies, owls and the super cute capybaras.

If you are so inclined, there is also a roller coaster. Amusingly known to locals as 'Japan's slowest roller coaster', it speeds past at a blistering 13.7km.

Entry 800 yen, all access pass 1800 yen • 9am-5pm • Closed on Tuesdays

2) Adachi Fisheries Market

Unlike the former Tsukiji Market and its replacement, Toyosu Market, Adachi has largely escaped the crowds due to being rather away from anything else of interest to tourists. Local vendors are therefore much more welcoming to visitors.

On some second Saturdays of the month the market floor is open to visitors, but check at your hotel or an information center beforehand. Unlike the other markets mentioned, you can actually walk around the market floor and take videos and photos, rather than being confined to observation decks. You'll be able to see workers darting around on their little mobile vehicles, auctioning big tuna and using mega machinery to cut up the frozen fish.

On other days of the month, you'll still be able to indulge yourself at the associated seafood restaurants. You'll also be able to pick up fresh vegetables, fruits and dried produce from the market, at much better prices than a convenience store.
Free • 8am-10:30pm • Closed on Sundays

Meeting the friendly folks at the fish market

3) Ishihama-Jinja
Dedicated to the deity of longevity, Japanese people visit this shrine to pray for good fortunes.

One rather odd part is the 'fujizaka'. A leftover from a Mount Fuji cult, it's a mound of rocks that was taken from the base of Fujisan. It was believed that ascending the fujizaka was the spiritual equivalent of climbing the real thing.
Free • 9am-4pm

4) Mukojima-Hyakkaen Gardens
The 'Hyak' in the name refers to 100, and the goal of this Japanese garden was to create an oasis with a hundred flowers that bloom throughout the four seasons. The only surviving flower garden from the Edo period, many people flock here for plum trees when they bloom, typically in February and March.
150 yen • 9am-5pm

5) Tokyo Skytree
With all the new skyscrapers popping up over the last few decades Tokyo Tower was just not tall enough anymore, and a new broadcast tower was needed. Tokyo Skytree was constructed, and at a height of 634 meters is currently the tallest tower in the world. The neofuturistic design and computer-animated illuminations at night really make this tower stand out from all the rest.

At the base of the tower is Tokyo Solamachi, a huge shopping mall. The number of shops is just astonishing, and there are all sorts of fun themed areas. The Japanese Souvenirs area (4F) has loads of unique gifts on sale, the Japan Experience Zone (5F) has some very Japanese interactive games and experiences, while Fashion Zone (2F) has plenty of tax-free clothing shops.

There are also some 'character shops', offering toys and souvenirs based around your favorite anime and manga characters.
500 yen • 10am-5pm • Closed on Mondays and Tuesdays (except national holidays)

Recommended cafe
Part of Ishihama-Jinja, Raku Ishihama Teahouse is a convenient spot along the route. If it's a cold day, there will be nothing better than some matcha tea accompanied by some sticky rice balls. Light tempura rice bowls and katsu sets are also available.
Drinks and snacks from 300 yen, meals from 800 yen • 11:30am-8pm

Recommended meal spot
Grab an authentic, juicy burger at &Burger, just outside Arakawa Amusement Park. Known for their epic sizes, some of the burgers are towering in size, packed with loads of fillings and sauces.
1000-2000 yen • 11:30am-6pm • Closed on Tuesdays

Looking across Sumida River

Ueno Park to Yanaka Ginza – Ueno and Nippori
DISTANCE: 4 KM | BEST ON WEEKENDS, EITHER ON FOOT OR BIKE

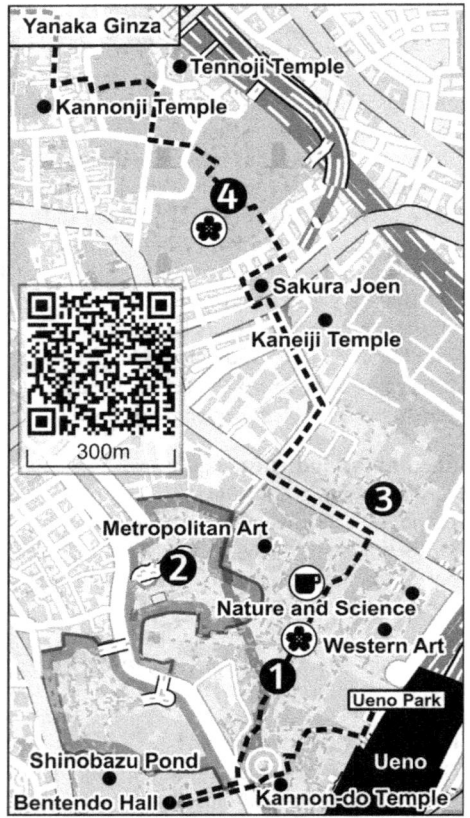

This walk traverses two quite different spots in east Tokyo. Ueno Park is a real treasure trove of tourist spots, featuring several museums, as well as various shrines and temples. On the other end is Yanaka, one of the few remaining old school shopping streets that is still to this day a bustling hive of activity. Be sure to start early if you want to give yourself enough time to enter every attraction, as well as queue up for any of the more popular animals at the zoo (this is the one with pandas!).

Starting and ending points

The best place to start from is JR Ueno Station (Ueno Park Exit). This is on various JR lines, but you can also access it on the Tokyo Metro, via the Ginza and Hibiya lines. The path then ends at Sendagi Station on the Tokyo Metro.

Places of interest

1) Ueno Park
On most Tokyo travel itineraries, you could easily spend a day just exploring all that is on offer. The park also draws in over two million people each year for cherry blossom viewing, but has a bunch of indoor things to do, so is great whatever the season or weather.

You're particularly spoiled for choice when it comes to museums in the park. The **Tokyo Metropolitan Art Museum** has one of Japan's best selections of fine art and sculptures (free, 9:30am-5:30pm), the **National Museum of Nature and Science** has cool 360-degree movies on dinosaurs and evolution (320 yen, 9am-5pm), and the **National Museum of Western Art** which houses art from the likes of Picasso and Van Gogh (500 yen, 9:30am-5:30pm).

Be sure to follow the route over to **Bentendo Hall**, a unique temple in **Shinobazu Pond**, on the park's west side. The pond has also been cultivated as a habitat for cormorants, medium to large sized birds that are expert divers. They used to be common across Japan, but are now endangered. *Park entrance free (special exhibitions may have extra fees) • 5am-11pm • Museums closed on Mondays (except national holidays)*

2) Ueno Zoo
The longest running zoo in Japan, and considered by most to be its flagship. It houses major draws such as pandas and gorillas, as well as rare species such as pygmy hippos. The new pandas, Ri Ri and Shin Shin, arrived in 2011.

While the novel monorail is sadly gone, the grounds are home to over 3,000 animals from 400 different species. Visitors can also

get up close in areas such as 'Gorilla Woods', 'Tiger Forest' and the small mammal house.
600 yen • 9:30am-5pm • Closed on Mondays (except national holidays)

3) Tokyo National Museum
This museum sometimes feels like it has it all. Over 300 paintings, sculptures, pieces of archaeology and calligraphy are on display in the main exhibition.

Special exhibitions in recent years include one on Okinawa, Japan's southern island that used to be part of the Ryukyu Kingdom, a kimono exhibition, and one on treasures from the early years of Buddhism in Japan. There is also **ColBase**, a collection of pieces from the other national museums in Kyoto, Nara and Kyushu.
1000 yen • 9:30am-5pm • Closed on Mondays (except national holidays)

4) Yanaka Cemetery
Stroll through this peaceful, at times beautiful cemetery. Inside there are lots of little temples, local cats walking around and a line of cherry blossom trees running through the middle. For those with an interest in Japanese history, you'll come across the graves of prestigious painters, actors, authors and statesmen from the Meiji era. Just before the entrance you'll also come across **Kaneiji**, a temple dating back to 1625 with a grand pagoda and many mysterious statues.

5) Asakura Museum of Sculpture
Pop in here if you're doing good on time with your walk or cycle ride. The former studio and school of Asakura Fumio, it housed award winning sculpture artists from the Meiji, Taisho, and Showa eras. Inside is a wide range of bronzes, tomes, paintings and pottery by Asakura and his students. There is also a Japanese roof garden and a carp pond, classic elements of a stately residence from these eras.
500 yen • 9:30am-4:30pm • Closed on Mondays and Tuesdays (except national holidays)

6) Yanaka Ginza
Escape back to the old Shitamachi (literally downtown) in this traditional shopping street, popular with domestic and foreign tourists alike. Along the way you'll see spots like **Shinimonogurui** (weekends, 12am-5pm), where you can get your own amusing name stamp, colorful sweets and pottery at **Yuzuriha** (10am-7pm) and **Niku no Suzuki** (10:30am-6pm, closed Mondays and Tuesdays), which sells delicious Japanese croquette. It's more of a post-war retro neighborhood, a place where locals still do their everyday shopping, while Tokyo weekenders come for a treat or two.

Recommended cafe
The Starbucks located in the heart of Ueno Park has become rather famous, and has recently been refurbished. The menu might be the same as elsewhere, but this Starbucks has a lovely park view from the open terrace.
Drinks 320-500 yen • 8am-9pm

Recommended meal spot
Grab some premium Wagyu beef burgers at Museca Times. Using only local ingredients to create both classic burgers as well as Japanese inspired ones, this new spot is quickly gaining a following in the area.
Burgers from 1400 yen • 11am-12pm (until 4:30pm on weekends • Closed on Wednesdays

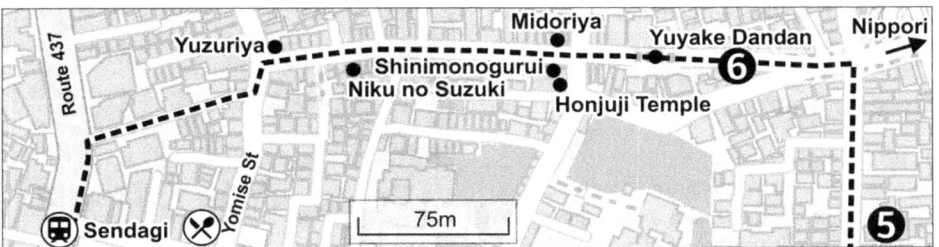

Nerding out for the day – Akihabara

DISTANCE: 1.5 KM | QUICKEST AND SAFEST ON FOOT

While Akihabara first made a name for itself as a major postwar black market, it has now solidly taken the post as the heart of techie Japan. There's something for anyone with a bit of geekiness in them, from cosplay cafes and gaming, to anime and manga. Let out your 'otaku' spirit in the town they call Akiba!

Starting and ending points

This circular route starts and ends at Akihabara Station (Electric Town Gate). Akihabara is on the JR Yamanote Line, as well as the Tokyo Metro.

Places of interest

1) Radio Kaikan
Twelve floors of action figures, TV character merchandise, models trains and cosplay gear. This Akihabara institution is jam-packed with geeky goodness. Just remember you'll have a few more hours of walking around the shops, so try not to use your wallet if you can. *10am-8pm*

2) Akihabara Gamers
Another chaotic megastore, this time devoted to manga and anime, plus related toys, trading cards and video games. The eighth floor often has events on, such as with manga authors, voice actors or anime directors. *10am-10pm (until 9pm on weekends)*

3) Main street
Heading up this road you'll soon pass a few gaming arcades, with among them some **GiGO** branches from Sega (10am-11:30pm), **Taito Station** (10am-11pm) and **Tokyo Leisureland** in **Don Quijote** (10am-1am). Older games still tend to be 100 yen, but more modern games, especially with custom hardware, can start from 200 yen.

You'll also come across lots of electronic and appliance stores, catering to any kind of need. Biggest is the **Bic Camera** store (10am-9pm), but shop around and hold your wallet for potential deals later on in the day.

Janpara (11am-7:30pm) is an excellent store for second-hand computers, parts and smartphones. Also worth a look is one of the **Suruga-ya** stores (9am-10pm), stocked with an array of board games, plastic models, little robots and lots of other goodies.

The main street of Akihabara

4) Gachapon Hall

Gachapon are a popular variety of capsule toy machines in Japan. Products are often of a higher quality than you might be used to abroad, with a range of prices, but there is some randomness to the exact toy that it will dispense.

You'll see them spread around Akihabara, but Gachapon Hall is the most well-known spot. It has around 500 machines, with a majority of toys aimed at grown-ups rather than kiddies.
11am-8pm (until 7pm on Sundays)

5) Akihabara Junk Street

Making our way down the narrower streets of Akihabara, you'll mainly start to get away from the chains, apart from a few dedicated to the otaku. Prices may be better, and there is a possibility of bargaining if you buy lots in one store. There's a shop for any taste or genre, whether for new or used items.

Favorites include toy store heaven **Kotobukiya** (12pm-8pm) and the 100-yen store **Can Do** (10am-9pm), but there are bargains to be had all along this street. It's also a perfect area to search for collectables and items not being manufactured any more.

Akiba Cultures Zone (11am-11pm), while a vast maze that's easy to get lost in, is considered a go-to place for all things anime. The same goes for the **Mandarake Complex** (12pm-8pm), which also has a bunch of collectables for manga, video games and retro franchises.

For gamers there's also a Dragon Quest themed **Lawson** convenience store (24h) with a load of merchandise related to the game. **Super Potato** (11am-8pm) will also be a must-see, as it contains a few floors of vintage games, plus an old school arcade.

6) LOAX

Boasting of being Tokyo's largest duty-free store, LOAX has a bit of everything that you might want to take home. This LOAX also caters to otaku with games, toys and other hobby goods. The multilingual staff make shopping here a breeze.

Onoden (10am-8pm), next door, has more choice of electronics and computers.
11am-7pm

Recommended cafe

Walking around you'll see at least a few dozen maids and cosplay-wearing waitresses trying to get you into their cafe. Once inside, the adorably dressed maids perform live shows, serve cute foods, play games and take commemorative photos with their customers.

Safe bets for first timers include **@Home Cafe** (11am-10pm), **Maidreamin** (11:30am-11pm), the more sophisticated **Cure Maid Cafe** (11am-8pm) and the cat loving **Akiba Zettai Ryoiki** (12pm-8pm). Feel free to ask the maids outside for English menus before entering, if you are unsure.
Cover charges 500-1000 yen, drinks and photos around 500 yen

Recommended meal spots

Try out Japan's take on Neapolitan pasta at **Spaghetti no Pancho** (11am-10pm, 760-1000 yen). It's a mile away from the real thing, but the main draw here is the mega sizes and toppings. A popular spot for salarymen.

A more upmarket alternative is **Roast Beef Ono** (11am-11pm, 1000-2000 yen). This restaurant serves rice bowls topped with tender Wagyu beef and raw egg.

Combine with...

Ueno (p34) is a short train ride north, and the same goes for Tokyo Station (p16) to the south. If you don't need too much shopping time in Akihabara, you should be able to do two in one day.

Checking out the electronics

From the heights of money to the heights of power – Akasaka, Roppongi and the National Diet

DISTANCE: 7 KM | POSSIBLE ON FOOT OR BICYCLE

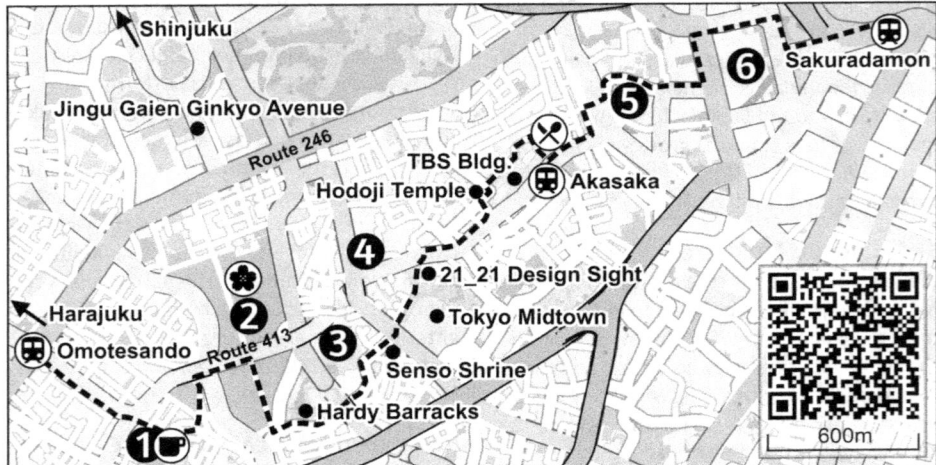

This route winds its way through some of the poshest shopping streets in Tokyo. Starting near Harajuku at Omotesando, it then gives a peek at Roppongi, a spot popular with wealthy foreigners, before heading through Akasaka, home to countless high-class restaurants. You'll then end up at the grand government district, or you could just finish at the Harry Potter Cafe and splash out there!

Starting and ending points

First, get on the Tokyo Metro Ginza, Hanzomon or Chiyoda line and make your way to Omotesando. It's only one stop from Shibuya or Meiji-jingumae (Harajuku). Leave from Exit A5 and walk down the right side of the main road. The walk then finishes at Sakuradamon, on the Yurakucho subway line.

Places of interest

1) Nezu Museum

An exhibition of pre-Modern Japanese and East Asian art from the collection of Nezu Kaichiro, the former president of Tobu Railway, one of Tokyo's major private railway companies. His aim was never to keep his collection private, a bonus for us all, and the main exhibition includes seven official National Treasures. He amassed more than 7,000 pieces of art using his vast wealth, from calligraphy to bamboo craftwork and ancient armor. The modern, easy to navigate building is a perfect place to display it all. Check out nezu-muse.or.jp for the current list of special exhibitions.

1300 yen • 10am-5pm • Closed on Mondays (except national holidays)

2) Aoyama Cemetery

Japan's first public cemetery, opened all the way back in 1874. It contains the graves of some of the capital's most historically and culturally significant people, as well as foreigners from the Meiji era (1868-1912). It's open to the public, so have a stroll around and see what you come across. It notably includes the grave of Hachiko, the famous Shibuya dog that waited for his owner every day outside Shibuya station, even for years after his death. The cemetery is also a popular spot during the cherry blossom season.

Free • 24h

Hie Shrine

3) The National Art Center, Tokyo

Considered to be one of Japan's most important art spaces, the National Art Center is housed in a stunning glass building in the upmarket Roppongi area.

A variety of ever-changing exhibitions are on display. In the past there have been ones based on Greek and Roman mythological paintings, the fashion of Yves Saint Laurent and classical Japanese calligraphy, among others. You're therefore sure to find something of interest.

Free to 2000 yen (depends on exhibition) • 10am-6pm (until 8pm on Fridays and Saturdays) • Closed on Tuesdays

4) Nogi-jinja Shrine

Often used for exclusive corporate events or super expensive weddings, Nogi-jinja Shrine is a serene, well-maintained Shinto site with the sleek Roppongi towers in the background. On occasion ancient 'gagaku' court music can be heard at the Inner Shrine, plus the shrine sometimes holds a traditional ceremony to break open a sake barrel and wish for good luck. Flea markets are also held on the fourth Sunday of every month.
Free • 6am-6pm

5) Hie Shrine

Another very Instagrammable spot on this walk, especially the stairs lined with red torii gates, which are reminiscent of Fushimi Inari Taisha in Kyoto. It's also one of the few Shinto shrines that has outdoor escalators up to the top!

The shrine is popular with women and couples that are trying to get pregnant. A statue of a mother monkey and her child is said to bring blessings to women who are hoping to, or are currently, pregnant, so you'll see lots of people stroking or petting it for good luck. The shrine is what Japanese people call a 'power spot', so locals also come here to wish to find a good partner, to get married and to raise a healthy family after the birth of their children.
Free • 6am-5pm

6) National Diet Building

The building here is where both houses of the Japanese parliament meet. A German-style design using locally sourced materials, it was designed by the winner of a public design competition, Watanabe Fukuzo, after much behind-the-scenes wrangling between various government departments. If you want to check out the inside, free English tours can be arranged on weekday afternoons at shugiin.go.jp.

Recommended cafe

Nezu Cafe, located in the pristine Japanese garden at Nezu Museum, offers lovely seasonal views over its small Japanese garden. Note that entrance to the museum is required.
Drinks 650-750 yen • 10am-4:30pm

Recommended meal spot

The Japanese are real Potterheads, so opening the Harry Potter Cafe right in the heart of Akasaka was a guaranteed hit. It serves a host of Hogwarts inspired light meals, such as toasted sandwiches, Platform 9 3/4 Beans and a Simmering Cauldron Soup. There is also a well-stocked souvenir shop. Reservations are usually needed, especially on weekends, so check hpcafe.jp beforehand.
Meals 880-2585 yen • 11am-11pm

Combine with...

If after getting to the National Art Center you want to explore more of Roppongi, especially its art scene, you could combine this walk with the Roppongi Art walk (p44). Alternatively, you could do this route after the Shibuya to Harajuku path (p8).

That other big terminal on the Yamanote Line - Ikebukuro

DISTANCE: 3 KM | BEST ON FOOT

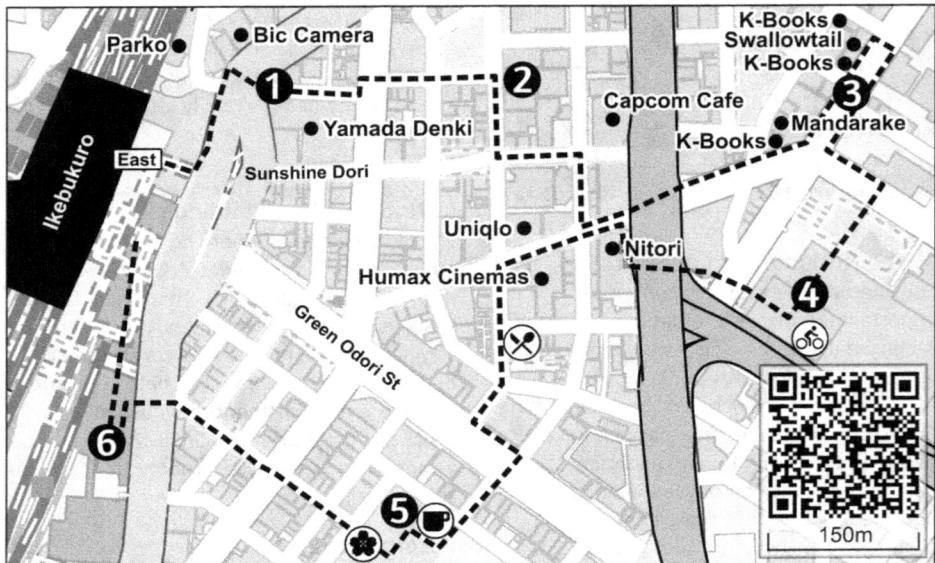

While not as cool and trendy as Shinjuku and Shibuya, Ikebukuro is slowly but surely turning the tide. It still feels very down-to-earth at points, with plenty of narrow streets to take a walk down, yet is also a convenient place to do a bit of shopping. You'll come across several department stores, mega malls and neighborhood stores, from the otaku (geek culture) to high-class brands. Tourists do come here, but not that many.

Starting and ending points

It would be possible to complete this path in either direction, but as Ikebukuro Station is a bit of a maze, starting from the East Exit and heading left is easiest.

Ikebukuro is on the JR Yamanote and Saikyo lines, as well as being a hub for the Seibu and Tobu railways. It's also on the Tokyo Metro's Fukutoshin, Yurakucho and Marunouchi lines. You'll end up at the Seibu department store, which has signage back to whatever train line you need.

Places of interest

1) Electronic megastores

Just to the north of the East Exit are **Bic Camera** and **Yamada Denki** (LABI). Video games, sake, SIM-free phones, computers and toys; both have several floors of all the techy wonders you'll need. They also have dedicated Apple sections, tax-free shopping and English-speaking staff on hand.
10am-9pm

2) Animate

Officially the biggest anime shop in the world. After receiving a major revamp in 2023, this store now features ten floors of geeky shops, cafes, event spaces and a theater. There are two floors dedicated to manga and related art supplies, as well as two more that focus on the most popular characters. The store also has a few nice extra touches, such as anime-themed drinks and cookies shaped like different franchise's characters.
11am-9pm (weekends 10am-8pm)

Cosplay on Otome Road

3) Otome Road

Akihabara (p36) is known across the world as the center of otaku culture, where anime and manga fans go in their droves. Otome Road is similar, but with the noticeable difference being that most of the stores focus on products for women rather than men.

It's all here, from fan-drawn comics to merchandise, plus many visitors enjoy cosplay (dressing up as their favorite characters). Major stores to check out include **Mandarake** (12pm-8pm) and the **K-Books** stores (12pm-8pm).

If you'd rather get served afternoon tea by handsome butlers, check out the **Swallowtail Cafe** (10:30am-9:15pm). Those that want to check out the **Evangelion Store** should head to Ikebukuro Parko, a small department store near to the electronics stores (11am-9pm).

4) Sunshine City

A huge shopping mall and commercial complex, with so much to offer. In terms of shopping, the site is home to the **Pokemon Center Mega Tokyo** (10am-8pm) and **Donguri Kyowakoku** (10am-8pm), which specializes in Studio Ghibli goods. **Sunshine Aquarium**, the first high-rise aquarium of its size in Japan, is perfect for kids with its penguin shows (1200-2400 yen, 10am-6pm).

There is also a planetarium from Japanese camera maker Konica (10:30am-9pm) and an indoor theme park called **Namjatown** (10am-10pm). On the 60th floor is an indoor park and observatory (700 yen, 11am-9pm).
Times vary according to the store, but usually 10am-9pm

5) Minami-ikebukuro Park

A modern park with a large lawn, making it perfect for a bit of a chill or as a spot to eat a bento. There are also a few cherry blossom trees and toilets, if you need them.
Free • 8am-10pm

6) Seibu Ikebukuro

The flagship department store of Seibu Railways, connected to the East Exit of Ikebukuro Station. Tax-free shopping can be enjoyed at over 100 brand stores, and there is also a Muji store on the south end.

Most impressive for tourists are the multiple food courts on the lower levels. There's a seemingly endless stream of both western and Japanese food stalls to roam around, so be sure to leave some space in your belly beforehand!
10am-9pm

Recommended cafe

Located in Minami-ikebukuro Park, grab a coffee at Cafe Racines Farm to Park and relax near the green lawn. This spot also puts on barbeques from time to time.
Drinks from 650 yen, waffles and meals around 1000 yen • 8am-10pm (from 9am on weekends)

Recommended meal spot

Mendokoro serves miso ramen at its best, and sure do the locals know it. The miso soup is thick and rich in flavor, and comes with chewy noodles and a choice of toppings. At lunch they frequently provide free rice bowls and vegetables. Come early on the weekend as there is usually a line.
Noodles 980-1340 yen • 11am-10pm

The busy streets of 'Bukuro'

From granny's Harajuku to milky hot springs - Sugamo
DISTANCE: 2.5 KM | BEST ON FOOT

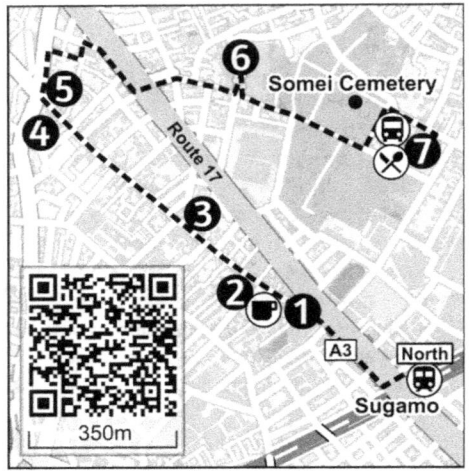

Sugamo is one of the smaller stops on the Yamanote loop line in Tokyo, located on the north side of it. It has a thriving shopping scene that is a mile away from the likes of Shibuya or Shinjuku, both in size and atmosphere.

This walk takes you up one of Tokyo's best traditional shopping streets, and in my opinion to one of Tokyo's best hot springs in which to soak your feet after an afternoon of walking and shopping.

Starting and ending points

If you are coming on the Toei Subway, the route begins from Sugamo (Exit A3) on the Mita Line. The north exit of JR Sugamo Station is also nearby.

You'll end up at Sakura Onsen, which has a free shuttle bus back to Sugamo (ask at the reception for times). Alternatively, you could walk south to Sugamo after the hot spring.

Places of interest

1) Sugamo Jizodori Shopping Street
Located along the Old Nakasendo Road, one of the five ancient roads of Japan. It was an important route connecting the western and eastern parts of the country, and while it no longer has any such use, this part has in modern times taken on a life of its own.

Known to locals as 'Harajuku for grannies', the street is incredibly nostalgic. Lined with old-fashioned clothing stores, noodle restaurants and Japanese confectionery stores, Jizodori makes for a great bit of souvenir shopping. Of particular fascination to older generations are the red items on sale, the color of which is said to symbolize vitality and happiness. It's the kind of shopping street where shopkeepers will be chatting away with their customers, giving the place a real non-corporate, friendly atmosphere. Expect to see the area really bustling on weekends.

2) Kintaro-ame
One of the more famous Japanese sweet shops on Sugamo Jizodori Shopping Street. It's super fun to explore this shop, and check out the retro, and often cute, candy. The store has been making sweets for almost seven decades, and there are more than 50 different flavors to try out. Many feature the face of Kintaro, a Japanese folk story character. It's one of several such shops on the street, so feel free to take your time browsing.
9am-6pm

Old fashioned establishments in Sugamo

The entrance to Jizodori

3) Maruji
One of the better-known stores where everything is red, from socks and underwear to funny souvenirs. It boasts of being Japan's first and top seller of red underwear, so check it out for an amusing bit of window shopping.
10am-5:45pm

4) Sugamo Yu
A neighborhood spa (called a sento) that was recently refurbished. Inside are all the essentials, such as an indoor bath, jet bath, electric bath and sauna. It may not be as feature-filled as the Sakura Onsen mentioned below, but it still feels modern and clean.
500 yen • 3pm-12am (from 12pm on Sundays) • Closed on Tuesday

5) Sarutahiko Okami
A rest stop along Nakasendo Road during the Edo era. The monkey god Sarutahiko is worshiped at this little neighborhood shrine, squashed in between business blocks.
Free • 24h

6) Honmyoji
On March 2nd, 1657, the Great Fire of Meireki destroyed the majority of Edo. For many years it was said that Honmyoji was the origin of this fire, though some believe it was forced to take the blame by the Shogunate rulers. Inside are the graves of figures such as Chiba Shusaku, a legendary Edo swordsman, and Toyama Kagemoto, a samurai from the same era. After Honmyoji, you'll pass through **Somei Cemetery**.
Free • 7am-5pm

7) Sakura Onsen
A modern hot spring, perfect for first timers and onsen fans alike. Sakura Onsen uses water gushing out from 1,800 meters below ground, quite rare in central Tokyo, where most 'hot springs' just heat up imported hot spring water, or simply warm up water from the taps. The water is therefore rich in natural minerals, with an amber tint and silky smooth to the touch.

Heated rock rooms and tatami relaxation areas, as well as massage chairs are available. As a pleasant touch, the 'silk milk bath' becomes a 'pink sakura bath' in spring.
1320 yen • 10am-11pm

Recommended cafe
Croquette Korokya has a wide selection of Japanese croquettes. Popular choices include juicy mince katsu, gratin, and beef, but there's also the rather adventurous-looking donut croquette. The quality is definitely better than buying from a supermarket.

Tully's Coffee, next door, is a popular cafe chain in Tokyo that has seating. Check the outside posters for the seasonal specials.
From 150 yen • 11am-7pm

Recommended meal spot
The restaurant at Sakura Onsen is a delight. A little Japanese garden with a koi pond outside, tatami floors and peaceful stones, it comes highly rated by anyone that tries it out. Inside you can order both classic Japanese 'teishoku' meals, as well as pastas and seasonal fare. If you are not up for the hot spring, it's possible just to visit the restaurant.
Meals around 1000 yen • 10:30am-11pm

An example of the Kintaro-ame offerings

Tokyo's essential art and museum walk – Roppongi

DISTANCE: 5 KM | BEST ON FOOT AND NOT ON TUESDAYS

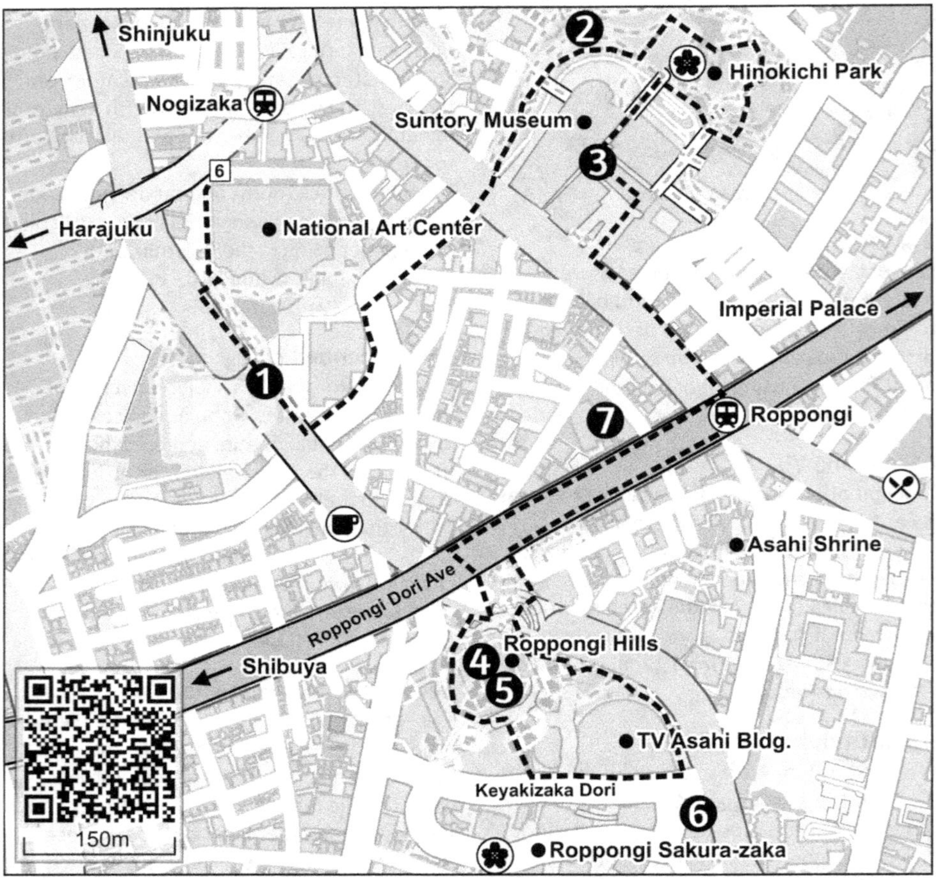

Roppongi, famous as the area where many wealthy foreigners, as well as Japanese celebrities, live and party in, has transformed itself into a center in recent times. All this money has led to several grand shopping and culture complexes, with a plethora of art galleries and museums to explore.

Starting and ending points

The walking route begins at Nogizaka Station on the Tokyo Metro Chiyoda Line. Depart from Exit 6 and head south towards Route 319 and the National Art Center, which is also on the Akasaka to National Diet path (p38).

You'll then finish at Roppongi Station, on the Tokyo Metro Hibiya and Toei Subway Oedo lines.

The Zipper

Places of interest

1) Roppongi Tunnel wall art
Even after visiting Roppongi many times over the years, it took a while before bumping into this hidden gem. Five oversized, eye-catching murals adorn the once dull walls of this underpass. There's quite a playfulness in them, such as in Jun Kitagawa's huge 'Zipper', and some require you to walk close up before you can realize what they truly depict. Get Instagram on the ready….

2) 21_21 Design Sight
A collaboration between three icons of modern Japanese design; designer Issey Miyake, graphic designer Taku Satoh and product designer Naoto Fukasawa. The aim of this institution is to create a space that shows off fresh ideas and perspectives on design and architecture, with most exhibitions focusing on everyday life. The little gallery opposite the entrance often has something free on too, so pop in there if the general entrance fee seems too much.
1200 yen • 10am-7pm • Closed on Tuesdays

3) Tokyo Midtown
Once you get to Tokyo Midtown, it might be hard to leave. It really does feel like a self-contained little city, housing everything from corporate offices and shopping to a Ritz-Carlton hotel and posh restaurants. If you are just here for culture though, first head to the **Galleria**. On the third floor, it has some of the most expensive yukata, geta (traditional shoes) and Japanese hand fans you'll likely see.

After this, continue to the **Suntory Museum of Art** (10am-6pm, closed Tuesdays, 1500 yen). The Suntory crew have built up a mega collection of fine art pieces, acquiring them since the 19th century. Recommended for lovers of traditional Japanese art, the museum has roving exhibitions ranging from lacquerware to glass, and Japanese scrolls to ceramics.
Main building 7am-9pm

4) Mori Art Museum
Arguably Roppongi's leading museum, located high up on the 53rd floor of the Roppongi Hills Mori Tower. Billing itself as a contemporary art museum with a focus on Asian artists, it prides itself on pushing boundaries in visual arts and design. Some of art's biggest names have been here, including Ai Weiwei, Gohar Dashita and Bill Viola.
From 2000 yen (200 yen off if you book via art-view.roppongihills.com • 10am-10pm (until 5pm on Tuesdays)

5) Tokyo City View
An indoor observation deck approximately 250 meters high, plus a rooftop deck 270 meters up. As you'll by now expect, the observation deck has cultural events and a gallery space, but the wonderful nighttime views are the real catch here.
From 2000 yen (200 yen off if you book via art-view.roppongihills.com) • Indoor 10am-10pm, rooftop 11am-8pm

6) Roppongi Tsutaya Books
Super hip bookstore with a pop-up space, lots of artsy coffee table books and innovative gift products. It seems just as much of a hang out spot for locals as a bookstore, and a place where you'll hear multiple languages spoken at once. If you are just browsing, it's perfectly fine to just stand about and read books for free, or you can grab a cup of coffee and read at a table.
7am-11pm

Interesting outdoor art at Roppongi Hills

Recommended cafe

Gallery & Cafe Camelish does a gallant job of exhibiting lesser known artists and creators, with new art put up on display every three weeks. It has light Asian lunches and a wide selection of teas and cocktails, set in a bright, colorful dining room.

Food 1000-1500 yen, drinks from 590 yen • 11:30am-10pm (until 5pm on Mondays) • Closed on Tuesdays

Recommended meal spot

Want to try a twist on udon, the thick Japanese noodles? Tsuru Ton Tan features hilariously huge bowls of the stuff, with inventive and delicious sauces and toppings. Challenge yourself and try something like curry soup noodles with pork katsu on top, or a massive carbonara bowl.

Bowls 1000-2000 yen • 11am-12pm (until 4:30pm on weekends) • Closed on Wednesdays

What you'll see from the Tokyo City View

Upmarket and historic shopping heaven – Ginza

DISTANCE: 3 KM | BEST ON FOOT DUE TO CROWDED STREETS

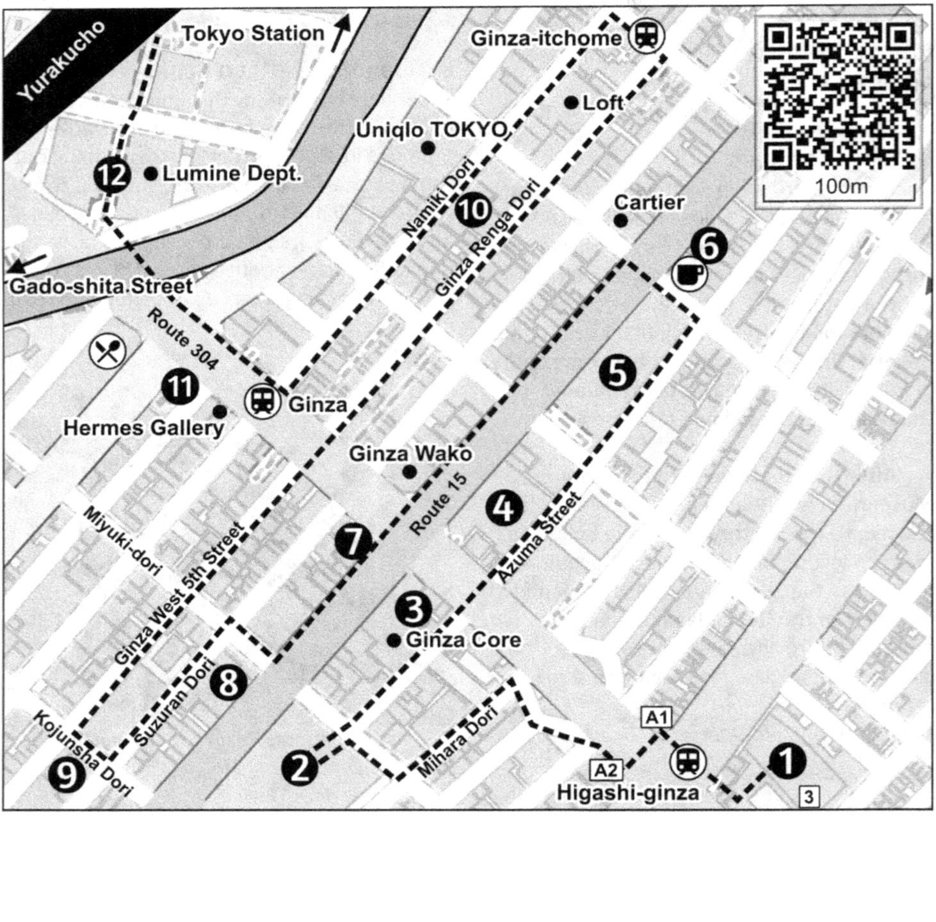

Ginza was Tokyo's first Western-style shopping district, and still to this day houses all of the main luxury department stores, plus a few extra. It's where the super-rich have been coming for years to splash their cash. For average folks there's still plenty to do though, whether it's tax-free shopping or checking out free galleries. This walk will zig-zag you around the highlights.

Starting and ending points

First make your way to Higashi-ginza station, which is conveniently connected to Kabukiza (Exit 3), the first tourist destination. It's on the Hibiya and Asakusa lines. You'll then end up near Yurakucho Station, on the Yamanote and Tokyo Metro Yurakucho lines.

Places of interest

Tokyo's premier Kabuki theater

1) Kabukiza

Kabuki is a classical theater artform that combines traditional dance with drama. Featuring beautiful costumes and some very Japanese sets, the male-only performers make a strong use of body language and color to express themselves in the story. It really feels like an out of this world experience to see.

It would make sense to start your walk with a performance. Normal tickets for a whole show are very pricey, so if you want to save money go for the single act tickets, called Makumi. They are more than enough for tourists who want to experience Kabuki in the flesh. Rentable English audio guides are also available, which will help you understand what is being said on stage. Check the schedule and book at kabukiweb.net. Tickets are usually also available on the day.

Afterwards, be sure not to miss out on the **Kabukiza Gallery**, on the fifth floor. Featuring props and costumes from years of performances, it puts the stories into a more understandable context.
800-2000 yen • 10am-9pm

2) Ginza Six

One of the latest additions to the growing list of luxury shopping hotspots in Ginza. Inside you'll find brands such as Vivienne Westwood, Dior and Fendi, among others. Even if you're not doing any shopping, the main hall features massive hanging art pieces, sometimes from the likes of Yayoi Kusama, plus there is a modern rooftop garden and a few little art displays dotted around.
10:30am-8:30pm

3) Ginza Place

Home to the global flagship showrooms of Nissan and Sony. The facade to this 11-story building holds 5315 aluminum panels, arranged in a latticework to resemble the 'sukashibori' technique used in traditional flower baskets and Japanese incense burners.
11am-8pm

Hanging wall art in Ginza Six

4) Mitsukoshi

The OG department store in Ginza, and the oldest surviving one in Japan. All the tax-free shopping you would expect, from fashion to toys. The slightly odd **Art Aquarium** inside

combines variously shaped fish-filled water tanks with light effects, sounds and fragrances (11am-7pm, 2300 yen).
10am-8pm

5) Matsuya Ginza
Recently refurbished to keep up with all the new shopping complexes, Matsuya is an amazing place to go window shopping. The food floor is one of the city's best.
10am-8pm

6) Itoya
The store of this centuries old paper mill offers a wide selection of stylish and very Japanese postcards, in addition to classy stationary and patterned paper.
10am-8pm

7) Kyukyodo
Old Ginza store, focusing on calligraphy goods, tea ceremony items and other arts and crafts products. Excellent place for souvenir shopping Japanese-style gifts.
11am-7pm

8) Uniqlo Ginza
The largest Uniqlo store in the world, spanning 12 floors of clothes, accessories and exclusive Ginza-only t-shirt designs.
11am-9pm

9) Ginza Graphic Gallery
The ggg, as it's known to cool people, likes to put on bold exhibitions focusing on local and international trends in graphic design.
Free • 11am-7pm

10) MUJI Ginza Flagship Store
MUJI is a nationwide retailer, specializing in minimalist apparel and home products. There are six levels of the stuff here, and of course another fancy art exhibition upstairs!
11am-9pm

11) Sony Park Mini
An experimental and avant-garde pop-up space is located underground, while a new Sony Park is being built above.
Free • 11am-7pm

12) Yurakucho
A business district near Ginza, with a way more laid back atmosphere and way cheaper prices. Walk down **Gado-shita Street**, an alleyway full of yakitori restaurants, stand-only bars and casual izakaya.

Recommended cafe
Indulge yourself with an afternoon tea at Bulgari Ginza Bar. The 14 little dishes, from Italian desserts to mini sandwiches, are presented together in minimalist boxes, with homemade jam and British tea.
Sets 5900-6500 yen • 12am-5pm

Recommended meal spot
Tokyu Plaza Ginza has a host of trendsetting restaurants and fancy bento/deli spots.
Meals 1000-3000 yen • 11am-9pm

Combine with...
Once you are at Yurakucho, why not take a train one stop north, or walk up, to explore around the Tokyo Station area (p16)?

Ginza's main road

The royal circuit – Tokyo Imperial Palace

DISTANCE: 7 KM | BEST ON FOOT (SOME SECTIONS OFF LIMITS TO CYCLISTS)

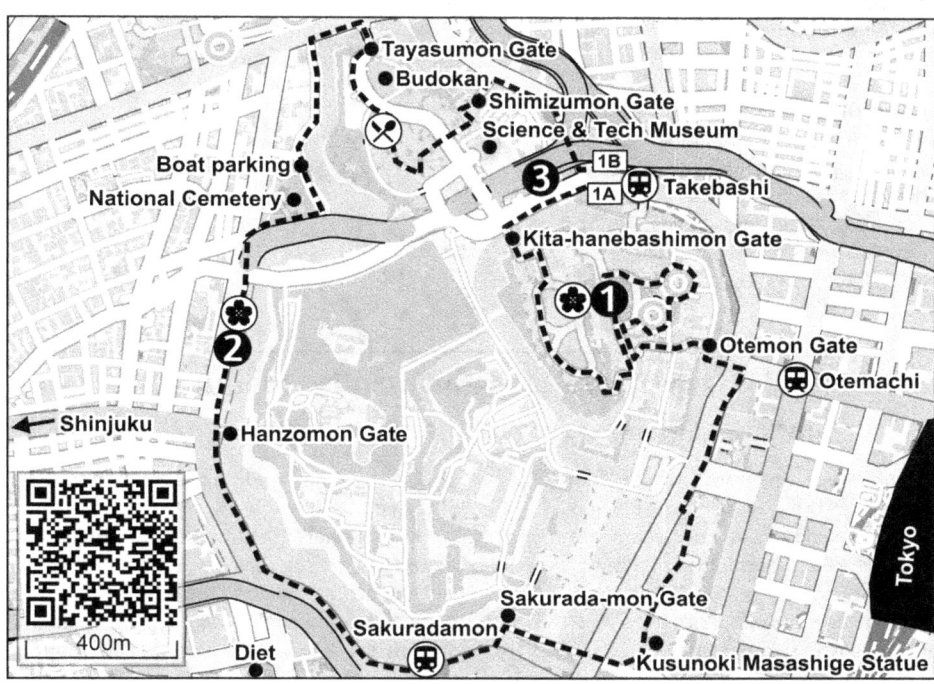

Hundreds of joggers and walkers make their way around the Imperial Palace every day, as part of their daily exercise. It's not just the perfect distance for such activities though, as the route is a visual delight the whole way. It is thought of by all Tokyoites as the quintessential walk in the capital.

The palace has served as the Emperor's home since 1868, before which it was a castle in the Edo period. Today it is surrounded by enchanting gardens, meticulously manicured lawns and intimidatingly grand stone walls and moats. While tourists are not allowed inside the buildings, there are a few spots where we can enter the grounds, so this route explores as much as possible.

Starting and ending points

From Takebashi Station (Exit 1A), walk over Takebashi Bridge to the west to begin the walk. The loop then finishes at this station.

Places of interest

1) East Gardens of the Imperial Palace

There's more than you'd expect here. As well as the usual Japanese garden elements there are old guardhouses where the high-ranking officials worked, an exquisite miniature of the Edo castle that used to be on the grounds, the remains of the main castle tower and a rare three-story keep that looks like a mini castle.

Be sure to also check out the Ninomaru Grove and Ninomaru Garden, a lush Japanese garden that's maybe as good as any other you'll see in Tokyo. Many people miss this area, and just focus on the castle and park.
Free • 9am-4:30pm (closed on Fridays and Mondays, or Tuesday if Monday is a holiday)

2) Chidorigafuchi Park

Opposite the British embassy, this park is particularly stunning in the cherry blossom season, with a 700 meter line of sakura trees,

but delights with striking views year round. A little further on visitors can also rent rowboats and enjoy exploring the moat.
Free (boats 500-800 yen) • Boats operate March to November (11am-5:30pm, 9am-8:30pm during the cherry blossom season)

3) National Museum of Modern Art
Masterpieces from both modern and classical Japanese artists, including the likes of Yokoyama Taikan, Kishida Ryusei and Fujita Tsuguharu. A craft museum is also next door.
From 500 yen • 10am-5pm (until 8pm Fridays and Saturdays) • Closed on Mondays (except national holidays)

Recommended meal spot
Situated in the outer garden, Cafe 33 offers posh pizzas, paninis and rice bowls, plus Hokkaido vanilla and Uji matcha ice creams. The concept of the cafe is to make you feel like you are taking a break in the forest.
Meals 800-1280 yen • 9am-5pm

Tokyo's best cherry blossom stroll – Meguro River
DISTANCE: 7 KM | BEST ON WEEKDAYS, TO AVOID THE CROWDS

Meguro River runs from Setagaya, via Meguro, all the way down to Shinagawa. While it developed as a rice paddy area during the Edo period, these days it's one of the most popular spots in Tokyo for cherry blossom viewing, or a quiet evening stroll outside of the sakura season.

Starting and ending points
From Shibuya take the Tokyu Toyoko Line to Naka-meguro, then take the East Exit and head to the river. You'll finish near Shimbamba Station, not far from Shinagawa. Due to the length of this route, you should use the below Google Map as you progress:

Places of interest
1) Cherry blossom viewing
For most of the route cherry blossom trees line both sides of the Meguro River, creating an almost ethereal tunnel of pink and white petals. While there will be some crowded spots, much of the river provides a mellow atmosphere that marks a contrast from most of the capital.

In total there is about one kilometer of sakura trees lining the river, with paper lanterns strung up along the way. Usually in bloom from the end of March to the middle of April, locals will come for a few beers and snacks from the food stalls that pop up, or bring their own and just soak it all in. The bridges that crisscross the river are perfect for taking photos.

When you do the path will make a big difference to your experience. For the most serenity, arrive early in the morning when only a few joggers will be out. After lunchtime the crowds will start to build up in the areas around the stations, but in between it may be better.

In the evening it's rather special though, if noisy at points. The thousand or so pink lanterns are lit up, and the reflection on the water surface is rather breathtaking.

2) Naka-Meguro Park
This community park is a good resting spot along the way. Why not do the classic Japanese things and grab yourself some sushi from the convenience store, sit down on the grass and enjoy the cherry blossoms?
Free • 24h

View from one of the bridges

3) Gotanda Fureai Waterside Plaza
Modern park, featuring a conveniently located Family Mart convenience store, with plenty of benches to take a break on. There are also some stairs down to lower areas of the river.
24h

5) Shinagawa Bridge
The point where you'll turn back to Shimbamba Station. Some of the stone wall from the Edo period can be seen, plus there are some traditional lantern pillars and resting posts. It's almost impossible to tell, but at this point on the river the Yamate Tunnel, a major expressway, actually runs under your feet.

6) Ebara Shrine
Established in 709, for samurai families to worship the 'Shinagawa Dragon God'. It may not be as well maintained as some you'll visit in Tokyo, but the dragon carvings and statues are pretty impressive. To locate the shrine, look out for the vermilion painted bridge as you head up the river.
Free • 24h

Recommended cafe
I'm Donut - yes, that's the shop's name - is a trending donut shop opposite Naka-meguro Station. Extremely fluffy and soft, there are classic flavors like chocolate and glazed, as well as more adventurous ones like prosciutto or pistachio. Note that after lunch time donuts start to sell out quickly, limiting your choice and eventually selling out.
Donuts 300-400 yen (electronic payment only - check before lining up) • 9am-7pm

Recommended meal spot
Hearty curry hot pots are the specialty at Hot Spoon. The curries are cooked for eight hours beforehand, providing a rich taste, then quickly served boiling hot in iron pots. It's all very customizable, with various vegetables, rice sizes (large is free!), soup bases and spiciness levels.
Sets around 1000 yen • 11am-11pm

Combine with...
The end station, Shimbamba, is only one stop or 30 minutes on foot from Kita-Shinagawa Station. From here you could start the cool canal walk around Shinagawa (p28).

Out in the Tokyo suburbs

Exploring the posh side of Tokyo – Jiyugaoka
DISTANCE: 3 KM | BEST ON FOOT AND ON WEEKENDS

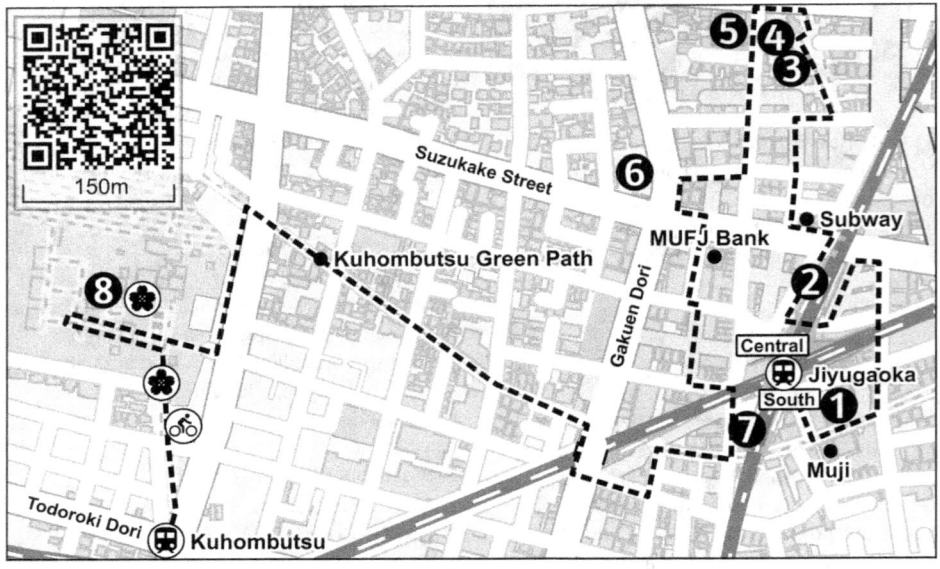

Jiyugaoka is possibly Tokyo's poshest suburban shopping and dining district, a maze of narrow streets dotted with trendy cafes, indie bakeries and fashionable boutiques. There's more than meets the eye though, and this walk will show some of the more interesting spots. Just forget about your bank balance for a few hours, and be prepared to splash out on some treats!

One of the cool streets in Jiyugaoka

Starting and ending points
The route begins from Jiyugaoka Station (South Gate), 15 minutes or so on the Tokyu Toyoko Line from Shibuya. You'll eventually reach Kuhombutsu Station, just one stop away on the Tokyu Oimachi Line.

Places of interest

1) Flipper's
The lines might have died down at this souffle pancake joint now that Instagram has moved on, but what remains is an excellent choice of the fluffy delights. Alternatively, try something healthier like an eggs benedict.
Pancakes 1300-1600 yen • 11am-7pm

2) Jiyugaoka Depart
Loads of teeny-tiny boutiques, recycle shops, bars and gift stores in a slightly dilapidated yet charming department store. It's a full-on

retro experience, culturally miles away from the hyper-trendy stuff you'll usually find in Jiyugaoka.
10am-8:30pm (closed on Wednesdays)

3) Kumano Shrine
Small shrine on the outskirts of town, with unclear origins. Head up through the long approach, via several torii gates, to reach the tranquil grounds and crimson painted main building. If you're looking for love, or more children, it's fun to also pick up a 'koi-mikuji' fortune slip. Get out Google Translate to find out what it says about your future!
Free • 24h

4) Kosoan
Charming little Japanese tea house that you could easily be excused for walking past unknowingly. Kosoan has a Zen garden at its back, and is a relaxing retreat for locals to enjoy some traditional, rather than modern, desserts. Inside are multiple tatami rooms with simple shoji sliding doors, and old fashioned instruments like shamisen on the walls. It really does feel like pre-war Japan.
Drinks around 1000 yen • 12pm-6:30pm (from 11am on weekends) • Closed on Wednesdays

5) La Vita
This small shopping zone is a slightly cheesy, but cute recreation of Venice. Inside it's all very Italian, and there's even a gondola floating on the canal. **Olor** serves classic Italian gelato (11am-7pm, around 450 yen) and **Cocomeister** (10am-7pm) is a classy little store selling leather goods.
9am-5pm

6) Today's Special
Jiyugaoka's posh take on the variety store. As you head in, the place does feel like a dream home. While some of the gourmet food is imported, much of it, as well as kitchenware, stationery and cosmetics, comes from local independent brands.
11am-8pm

7) BAKE the SHOP
Cheese tart heaven. These yummy delights, baked on site, are usually super fresh as the store tries to serve them within 30 minutes of baking. The limited edition tarts are always rather inventive and fun to try, whether it's a Mont Blanc Chestnut variety in autumn, or pumpkin and matcha for Halloween.
200-300 yen • 11am-8pm

8) Joshinji Temple
Relatively large temple that wouldn't seem out of place in Kyoto. Inside are buildings that have remained intact since the Edo period and three stunning Buddha statue halls, located in a tranquil wooded compound. Housed in the buildings are official Tangible Cultural Properties, such as a wooden Amida Nyorai sculpture and a silk-based picture of the temple master Kaseki Shonin.

You have two options when you are done. One is to walk down the leafy promenade to Kuhombutsu Station, or alternatively you could head east back to Jiyugaoka.
Free • 6am-4:30pm

Combine with...
The path of this route is actually really close to Tama River, so afterwards you could easily pick up a rental bicycle and start that cycling course (p56).

Ikegami is also on the Tokyu rail network, and if you manage to do Jiyugaoka in the morning then it would be possible to do both in a day (p58).

The entrance to Joshinji Temple

Akihabara for Japan travel addicts – Nakano

DISTANCE: 1 KM | BEST IN THE AFTERNOON

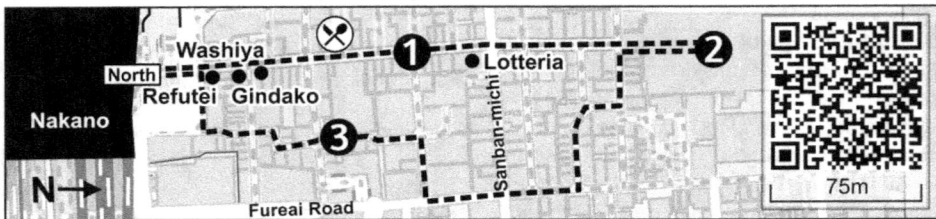

If you want to explore comics, rare figurines and other geeky delights, Nakano feels like a much more down-to-earth location than Akihabara (p36). It still brings the crowds in, but is far less commercialized.

Starting and ending points

Nakano is about six minutes on the Chuo Line from Shinjuku. The route starts and loops back at the North Exit.

Places of interest

1) Nakano Sun Mall

The main shopping arcade is a mixture of brand and independent stores. Just before entering is **Refutei** (11am-8pm). You'll want to get in line for their famous Obanyaki, stuffed pancake/sponge cakes.

As you make your way up you'll see **Gindako** (9am-9pm), a safe bet for trying out takoyaki, AKA octopus balls. You can mix things up with toppings like teriyaki sauce or a highball drink. Opposite is **Washiya** (9:30am-8pm), a traditional delicatessen that serves classic bento boxes.

Another highlight further up is **Lotteria** (7am-11pm), as this branch of the burger chain has a special 'Koala Pancake', which is similar to an Obanyaki but much cuter!

2) Nakano Broadway

This old-fashioned shopping mall is packed with manga, anime and game shops, as well as the odd maid cafe and the kind of video gaming arcade that in most cosmopolitan centers has been lost to time.

Highlights definitely include the **Mandarake** series of stores (12am-8pm). The main store focuses mainly on anime and manga, but the 30 or so little branches contain many genres of crazy knick-knacks and goods for almost any niche. It's all here from retro games to Kamen Rider. There is also the newer **Mandarake Henya** (4F), which has a large array of pre-war toys and signs.

It's a joy just to stroll randomly around the independent stores, but there are a few standouts. **Gaochi** (12pm-8pm, 3F) is packed from floor to ceiling with idol postcards, trading cards and masks. In the basement is **Daily Chico** (10am-8pm), which became popular on Instagram for its towering eight-flavor ice cream cones. Finally, **Fujiya Camera** (10am-8:30pm) is a must-see for camera lovers, holding more than 2,000 second-hand items, as well as new products. Note that many stores such as this one will offer tax-free shopping for foreign tourists.

3) Nakano backstreets

Head away from the main streets and you'll enter a treasure trove of alleyways and izakayas. While mainly geared towards local businessmen, it's an atmospheric place to come and take some pictures.

Recommended meal spot

Miso Ga Ichiban serves a wide range of ramen and tsukemen (dipping noodles), all served with the store's thick, rich miso based broth. It's a bit hidden away in a basement, so look out for the squiggly 味噌が一番 text.
Bowls 800-1000 yen • 11am-11:30pm

Jindai Botanical Gardens – Chofu

DISTANCE: 4 KM | BEST TUESDAY TO FRIDAY

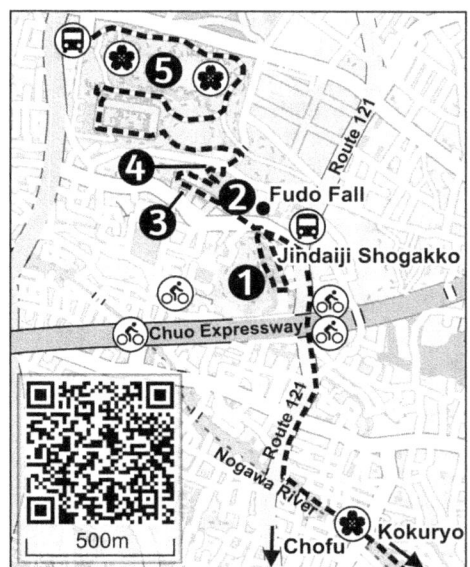

I hadn't heard of this spot until a number of years of living in Tokyo had passed, and what a delight it was to come across it by chance. The gardens, as well as the traditional shopping street and temples, remain very much a hidden gem in the suburbs of Tokyo.

Starting and ending points

First take the Keio Line from Shibuya in Tokyo to Chofu. Next, take a Jindaiji (no.34), Kichijoji (no.14) or Mitaka (no.66) bound bus and get off at Jindaiji Shogakko. The route then ends up on the west side, with buses back.

It's also possible to cycle or walk from Kokuryo Station, a few train stops away, via Nogawa River. This is particularly pleasant during the cherry blossom season when the river is lined with sakura trees.

Places of interest

1) Aquatic Botanical Gardens
While not as pretty as Jindai, this is a more relaxing spot to check out as very few people explore down here. It's where more of the aquatic plants are cultivated rather than shown off, and worth a free stroll around.
Free • 9:30am-4:30pm • Closed on Mondays (except national holidays)

2) Jindaiji Temple
The second oldest Buddhist temple complex in Tokyo, being founded in 733. Unblighted by the tourism that you get in central Tokyo, Jindaiji remains just as it was back in the olden times.

Visitors first walk up **Jindaiji Sando**, a traditional shopping street lined with soba restaurants and confectionery stalls, before being welcomed by the temple's 17th century gate. Inside, the temple is known as a sanctuary of peace and prayer, and you'll no doubt see Japanese people following the local rituals of Buddhist prayer.
Free • 9am-5pm

3) Jindaiji Tsukuri Shi
Interesting temple building containing humorous, as well as intricate, Buddhist statues.
Free • 24h

4) Jindaiji Pet Cemetery
Pet funerals are becoming more and more popular in Japan, with 400-500 being interred here each month. The cemetery contains hundreds of little pet vaults surrounding a 39 meter high **Tower of Souls,** with messages and tributes to the departed.
9am-6pm

5) Jindai Botanical Gardens
The main draw here. Home to the biggest rose garden in Tokyo, plus a wide variety of seasonal plants, you'll need at least an hour or so to explore all that's on offer. There's all the Japanese classics, such as wisteria, plum trees, cherry trees and peonies, plus tropical and subtropical plants in the greenhouse.
500 yen • 9:30am-5pm • Closed on Mondays (except national holidays)

Cycling the Tamagawa River – Kawasaki to Haijima

DISTANCE: 45 KM | BEST THURSDAY OR FRIDAY

The quintessential classic cycling ride in Tokyo. With a mostly flat route along dedicated paths, as well as multiple available start and finish points, it's perfect for any kind of cyclist. Along the way there are various 'power spots', from shrines to Japanese gardens, and even abandoned castle grounds.

Starting and ending points

From Shibuya take the Tokyu Toyoko Line to Shin-Maruko, about 18 minutes away, to begin. The route ends near Haijima Station, on the west side of Tokyo.

Where you start and end is completely customizable though. Train lines run along much of the river, with dozens of stations to pick up or drop off your rental bicycles. For example, you could finish at the Hugsy Doughnuts mentioned below and catch a train from the nearby Seiseki-Sakuragoaka Station.

Places of interest

1) Tamagawa Sengen Shrine

Originally built approximately 800 years ago, this hilltop shrine offers wonderful views over Tamagawa River, as well as the railway bridge crossing it. You'll even be able to see Mount Fuji on a clear day.

The local legend goes that during the early years of the Kamakura period (1192-1333), a warrior named Yoritomo went to battle in the Ikebukuro area. His wife, concerned about his life, went looking for him, but after injuring her foot she had to abandon her journey and seek help close to the river. After treatment, she was able to climb this hill to pray for her husband.

The wife eventually built a statue at the shrine called **Seikanzenon Bodhisattva**. The grounds also contain the copper statue of **Daibosatsu Bodhisattva**, which was excavated from the 5th station of Mount Fuji in 1652. Missing a leg at the time, it was brought to the shrine for repair and was enshrined here.
Free • 24h

2) Tamagawadai Park

Get off your bike and take a quick stroll at this beautiful public park, selected as one of the 'Eight Great Views of Tamagawa'. As you explore the many winding paths, you'll see gardens for aquatic plants, wildflowers and hydrangeas, plus ancient burial grounds dating back to the 4th century.
Free • 9:30am-5pm

3) Zen-yoji Temple

I had never seen a temple like this! Zen-yoji is a Buddhist temple littered with overwhelmingly big statues and stone artwork depicting everything from frogs to Hindu Ganesha. The artifacts come from across India and Asia, really setting this temple apart from others in the capital.
Free • 24h

The slightly intimidating entrance to Zen-yoji!

4) Futako-Tamagawa Park
Just outside the HQ of mega conglomerate Rakuten is this idyllic park. A sweet spot for a coffee break with its cafe, occasional food trucks and picturesque views over Tokyo. There's also **Kishin-en**, a compact Japanese garden featuring a 100-year old teahouse.
Free • 24h (Kishi-en 9am-5pm)

5) Fuchu City Local History Museum
Outdoor museum with old townhouses, farmhouses, a town hall and an elementary school building. These are filled with artifacts from the Meiji and Taisho eras, plus there is an exhibit about the history of the city and another about life in a wartime school. English language signage is limited, but it's still very interesting to take a look around.
9am-5pm • Closed on Mondays (except national holidays)

6) Takiyama Castle Ruins
Listed as one of Japan's top 100 castles, this 16th century site is completely unknown to most Tokyoites. While all that remains from the old era today are the remnants of moats and earthworks, there is an informative AR experience that visualizes what the castle would have looked like 500 years ago.
Free • 24h

7) Ishikawa Sake Brewery
Japanese sake brewery that started way back in 1863, and still uses the old Kura storehouses. It also started to brew beer for a short period in the 1880s, and revived this production with its Tama no Megumi brand in 1998. This beer, as well as sake, can be purchased in the onsite store to take home. There's also a sake museum.

Note that Ishikawa is one of the few to hold English-language tours in Tokyo. The guide will explain the sake making process, take you around the historic grounds and explain a bit about the giant bronze cauldron that was used to boil water for beer production.

Book your tour beforehand at tamajiman.co.jp. If you arrive too late for a tour, or tours are not available, it's also perfectly possible to explore much of the grounds on your own.
10am-6pm • Closed on Tuesdays

8) Akishima Onsen Yuranosato
Modern hot spring, with a classy yet understated feel, that comes with multiple indoor and outdoor baths. The 'one man' baths are particularly relaxing. Afterwards the onsite restaurant offers classic Japanese sets like ramen and soba.
850-950 yen • 9am-1am

Recommended cafes
There are a few spots along the way if you need a power boost. Daikokudo, near the beginning, is famous for its fish-shaped ayu sweets filled with red bean paste (11am-5:30pm, closed Tuesdays). At about the halfway mark Hugsy Doughnuts is an adorable neighborhood favorite (11am-6pm, Friday to Sunday), while Cafe Hikobae offers some top-rated riverside coffees (11:30am-5pm, closed Mondays and Fridays).

Recommended meal spot
Fussa No Birugoya, at the Ishikawa Sake Brewery, is an Italian restaurant offering local beer and sake, accompanied by handmade pizzas and pasta. If this seems too pricey you could indulge in some cheap conveyor-belt sushi instead. Sushiro is just around the corner (11am-11pm).
Meals from 1300 yen • 11:30am-9:30pm

Combine with...
This route finishes at Haijima, where the America Town walk begins (p66).

Cycling along the river

Ikegami's temples – Ota City

DISTANCE: 6 KM | SOME UPHILL SECTIONS, BUT OK FOR MOST PEOPLE

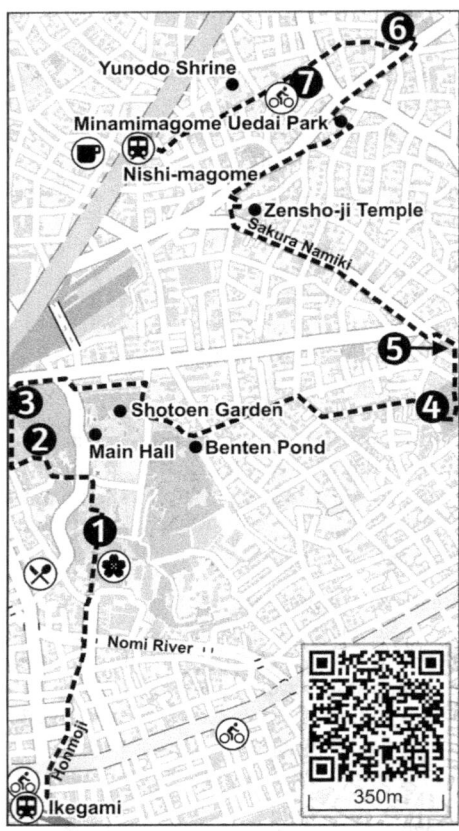

As Tokyo's main temples have become more popular with tourists, and many flock to the same ones, it can become hard at times to enjoy them. Thankfully, because of their locations, there are still grand temple complexes that escape the tour buses, and Ikegami Honmonji Temple is one of them. There is an abundance of amazing Buddhist architecture and history to be found in the Ikegami area, and taking a walk or cycle ride is a lovely way to experience it all.

Starting and ending points

From Gotanda Station, located on the Yamanote Line that loops around Tokyo, transfer to the Tokyu Ikegami Line. If coming from the east of Tokyo, take the JR Keihin-Tohoku line to Kamata and transfer there.

The walk starts from Ikegami Station (North Exit). Make your way through the shopping district north of the station and it won't be long until you reach the main temple area. The path then finishes at Nishi-Magome, on the Toei Subway, which can take you back to Gotanda.

Places of interest

1) Ikegami Honmonji Temple

This certainly isn't your average suburban temple, as the complex has a size of nearly 100,000 square meters. Give yourself at least half an hour to explore all that is on offer.

The prominent temple complex belongs to the Nichiren sect, a federation of four ancient Buddhist schools. Serving as a training and living quarters for aspiring monks, the grounds include a five-story pagoda that is regarded as one of the oldest in the Kanto region and was designated as an Important Cultural Property by the Japanese government.

The cherry blossom season in April is particularly beautiful, with pale pink blossoms scattered along the stone paths.
Free • 24h

Tahoto, at Honmonji Temple

2) Daibo Hongyoji
Said to be the place where the founder of the sect, Nichiren Shonin, passed away. Built on the site of a former mansion, there are some interesting temple halls, a Japanese garden and Myoho-do, where two goblins are enshrined!
Free • 9am-5pm

3) Ikegami Plum Garden
Originally the residence of Shinsui Ito, a Japanese painter, this garden has hundreds of plum trees, azaleas and cherry blossom trees. There should be something of interest whatever the season.
100 yen • 9am-4pm • Closed on Mondays (except in February and March)

4) Saikiyama Green Hill
A pleasant little community park, with a boardwalk up to commanding views of the area. There are also a few local historical ornaments, plus a restored traditional storehouse.
Free • 9am-5pm

5) Ryushi Memorial Museum
Established by Ryushi Kawabata, the founder of modern Japanese painting, the Ryushi Memorial Museum houses more than a hundred of his works. He was known as a painter in the 'Nihonga' style, which strictly used only traditional Japanese techniques and materials, rather than western-style styles that became popular in the Meiji period. It's definitely worth popping into, especially if you want to escape the summer heat for a bit.
200 yen • 9am-4:30pm • Closed on Mondays (except national holidays)

6) Manpukuji
A temple belonging to the Sodo sect, Manpukuji was built in the Kamakura period (1180-1336). Most impressive are the colorful sculptures of the 'four heavenly kings' and a grand statue of a Surusumi horse, all of which set this house apart from most.
Free • 7am-6pm (until 5pm October to March)

7) Ota City Local History Museum
A collection of historical artifacts, paintings and drawings from around Ota City, and exhibitions on the former seaweed farming businesses that used to inhabit the area. It's small and doesn't have much English, but it's a quaint little museum that's worth a quick visit.
Free • 7am-6pm (until 5pm October to March)

Recommended cafe
Located at the end of your walk or cycling ride, Cheval Cafe serves healthy, light meals. Family favorites include the demi-glaze 'hamburg' steak and rice, as well as the puddings served in cute mini clay pots. The outdoor decking, with cherry blossom trees, is the best place to get a seat.
Meals around 1250 yen, drinks and desserts from around 500 yen • 10am-3pm, 6pm-10pm (closed Mondays and Tuesdays)

Recommended meal spot
Located in a retro 1930s wooden house, Old House Cafe Rengetsu serves energy boosting meals like burgers and sandwiches, as well as a host of fancy rice dishes that are a mile away from cheap gyudon chains like Matsuya or Yoshinoya. The cakes are rather divine, and the coffee gets top marks too.
Meals 750-1100 yen • 11:30am-6pm

Honmonji Five-Story Pagoda

East Tokyo's underappreciated tourist spots – Koto City
DISTANCE: 5.5 KM | GREAT ANY TIME OF THE YEAR

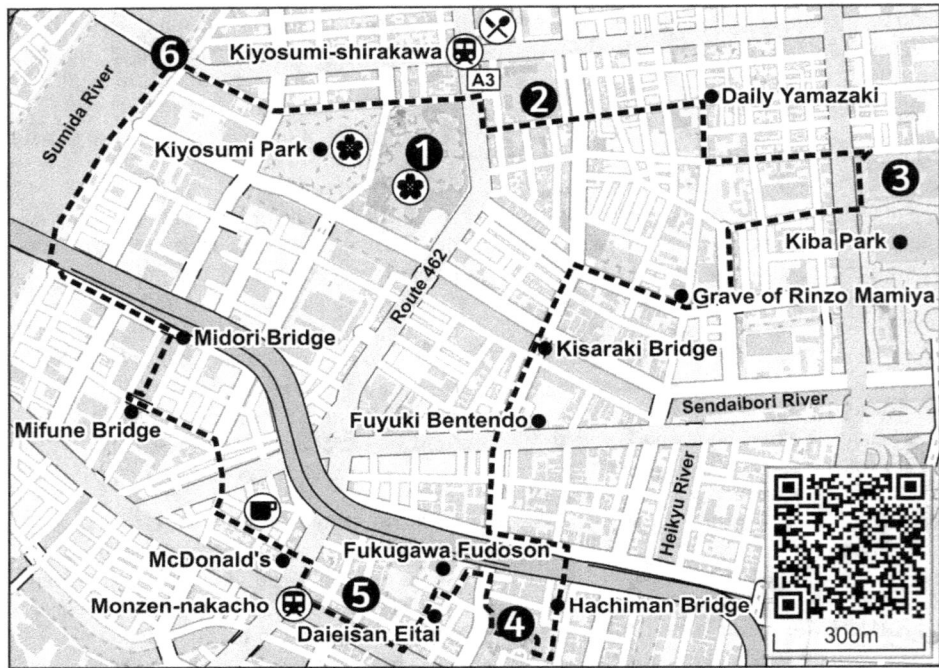

This area east of the Sumida River in Koto has much to offer, but it tends not to be a place many foreign tourists visit. One key reason why many people don't venture out here is that while it has a stunning Japanese garden, there are bigger and easier-to-access ones in the center.

This also applies to its history museum, modern art museum, and the same could be said about the shrines here. This path is a neat walk or cycling ride for someone who has been to Tokyo a few times already and/or wants a more lowkey but still exciting day of tourist spots.

Starting and ending points

Take the Toei Subway Oedo Line or the Tokyo Metro Hanzomon Line and get off at Kiyosumi-shirakawa (Exit A3). The entrance to Kiyosumi Gardens is well signposted.

This is a circular route, but if you've done enough walking or cycling at the halfway point you could finish at Monzen-nakacho Station, on the Toei Subway Oedo and Tokyo Metro Tozai lines.

Places of interest

1) Kiyosumi Gardens

It can feel too time-consuming to explore some of the Japanese gardens in Tokyo, with their vast grounds and multiple routes around. Kiyosumi Gardens is much more manageable, and still has the classic elements that you would want, such as a tea house, a large central pond surrounded by stone ornaments and crisscrossed with wooden bridges, and of course more than a few koi fish.

150 yen • 9am-5pm

2) Fukagawa Edo Museum

If you feel intimidated by the endless exhibits at Edo-Tokyo Museum, Tokyo's main history museum, then this is the place for you. The museum is set in a recently renovated, authentically recreated town based on the end of the Edo era (1603 and 1867). You'll be able to see exactly how people lived at the time, going into homes, seeing how they cooked and ate, and what kinds of jobs people were given. It's all indoors, but the museum's lighting changes to reflect the times of the day.

English-speaking volunteer guides can also take you on a tour, and have become real pros at explaining life back in the olden days.
400 yen • 9:30am-5pm • Closed on Mondays (except national holidays)

Inside Kiyosumi Gardens

3) Museum of Contemporary Art Tokyo
Voted one of the capital's best museums by TimeOut magazine, this is Japan's largest contemporary art museum, with work from both Japanese and international artists. The main hall has a rotating collection of 5,400 exhibits, and there are also special exhibitions on a variety of genres. See mot-art-museum.jp for what's currently on.
Prices depend on exhibition • 10am-6pm • Closed on Mondays (except national holidays)

4) Tomioka Hachiman Shrine
The largest of the Hachiman shrines in Tokyo, which are related to the god of martial arts and war. Visitors might also see robed priests performing safety rituals over cars parked here. It's one of the special services the shrine performs!

The next door **Fukagawa Fudoson** temple is usually more popular though. As you walk towards this you'll come across a line of little shrines that look like small log cabins, just behind the main shrine building.
Free • 24h

5) Monzen-nakacho
A traditional shopping area known for its waterfront vistas, cherry blossoms and interesting alleyways. The area is also known for Monozukuri, a Japanese concept that emphasizes a passion for technical know-how when creating artisan goods. You'll therefore pass many local shops selling off items that you won't find anywhere else.

6) Kiyosu Bridge
As you walk up Sumida River you'll be greeted by spectacular views towards the SkyTree. Come at night when the structure is lit up with animated displays.

Recommended cafe
Truffle Bakery has been trending quite a bit on Instagram, and for good reason. Most popular is the truffle salt bread, and the ever changing selection of curry bread will hopefully whet your appetite.
Breads 650-750 yen • 9am-7pm (until 6pm Saturday and Sunday • Closed Mondays

Recommended meal spot
Uminodon Donmaru is a cheap and cheerful seafood bento shop. Meals are delivered fresh, and quickly, making this spot hard to beat if you're in the mood for raw fish.
Bento boxes from 500 yen • 10am-9pm

Looking towards the Skytree

Nostalgia on Edogawa River – Shibamata

DISTANCE: 3 KM | BEST ON FOOT, ON WEEKENDS

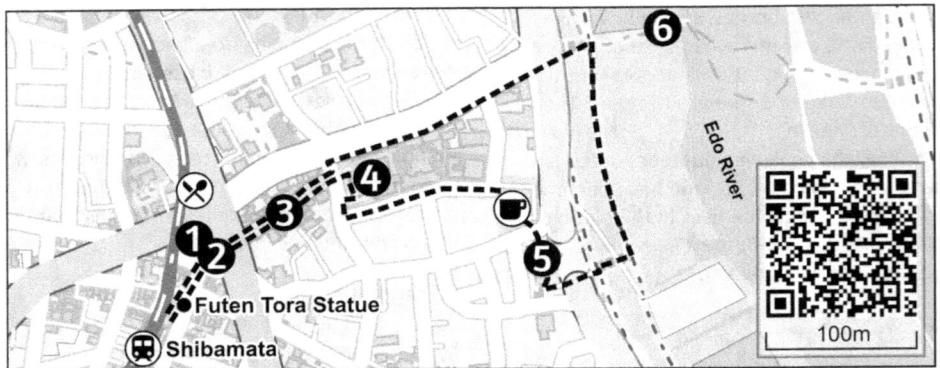

Shibamata, in Tokyo's Katsushika Ward, is a town mostly known as the setting for the movie series Otoko Wa Tsurai Yo, with an old-school downtown feel that worked perfectly on screen. Shopping streets dating back to 1912 still remain, and have been kept alive due to visiting movie fans, so it makes for an excellent afternoon walk.

Starting and ending points

The walk begins and ends at Shibamata Station on the Keisei-Kanamachi Line, just outside of central Tokyo. You'll probably need to come via Keisei-Ueno, with a transfer at Keisei Takasago. Alternatively, if coming via a JR line you'll need to transfer at Kanamachi.

Places of interest

1) Shibamata Toy Museum

Collection of vintage toys, including Japanese wooden dolls, teddy bears and model trains. Katsushika Ward actually used to have a concentration of toy makers in the early 1900s, with the area having a reputation as the place to go for cheap children's toys and candy. Pop in for some Showa-era snacks!
200 yen • 11am-6pm (weekends and holidays only)

The entrance to Shibamata Taishakuten

2) Haikara Yokocho

Continue your trip back in time along this shopping street, one of the last remaining in Tokyo to still have porcelain tiles on the road instead of concrete. It's a maze of retro pinball and arcade machines, snack shops and baseball card sellers.

3) Taishakuten Sando

The main street in Shibamata, lined with more traditional shops and a decent supply of food vendors. Top sellers include eel, toasted rice crackers and dango sweets (sticky balls on a stick made from rice flour). It's usually a few hundred yen per snack, so if you're a bit of a foodie Taishakuten Sando will be a real hit.

Inside Shibamata Taishakuten

4) Shibamata Taishakuten
Towards the end of Taishakuten Sando you'll come across Nitenmon Gate, which has been welcoming visitors to this temple since 1896, and an enormous pine tree.

Inside this temple complex are a host of intricate wooden carvings based on the life and teachings of Buddha, an inner garden and tatami rooms decorated with pre-war art and furniture. While you could just have a look from the outside, it's definitely worth paying the entrance fee to fully explore this place.
400 yen • 9:30am-5pm • Closed on Mondays (except national holidays)

5) Tora-san Museum
Find out more about the movie series that brought back life to Shibamata, as well as Tora-san, the movie's director. Basically, the movie is about a salesman struggling to make a living as he travels across the country, always longing to return to his far-away hometown of Shibamata. It became the longest running-movie series in the world, running between 1969 and 1995.

The museum shows off costumes and sets from the movie, such as a gyoza (dumpling) store and print shop, plus a man-powered tramway is on display. Even if you have never heard of the series, it's worth visiting for the glimpse you'll get into Tokyo of the 60s and 70s.
Free • 9am-5:30pm

6) Yagiri-no-watashi
The only remaining ferry on the Edogawa River. I say ferry, but this is really an arched wooden boat, the likes of which was regularly seen in the Edo period. Back then farmers had rice paddies on both sides of the river, and with no bridges needed such a service.

These days it's a cool little tourist attraction to try out, with most people doing a return trip, as there isn't much on the east bank. It's a rather peaceful endeavor being taken across, simply propelled by a rower.
200 yen • 10am-4pm (everyday March to November, then weekends only)

Recommended cafe
Yamamoto-tei is a restored teahouse providing real Japanese tea ceremonies. Constructed in the Sukiya-zukuri style, which emphasizes minimalist spaces that blend in with nature, there aren't many better places to try Japanese green tea. Kids, and big kids alike, can also drink Ramune, a carbonated drink popular at Japanese festivals. Drinks come with Japanese sweets or cookies, selected to compliment the taste of each other. The house also includes a local history museum.
Drinks 600-700 yen (museum admission fee 100 yen) • 9am-5pm

Recommended meal spot
Sepia is one of the better rated retro coffee spots in Shibamata. The walls are smothered with all sorts of knick-knacks and posters, with a menu that ups the nostalgia with items like cream soda and Japanese pudding. The pork curries are also a comfortable staple of homestyle Japanese cuisine.
Drinks 600-750 yen, meals around 1000 yen • 12am-5pm

Traditional stores in Shibamata

Showa Kinen Park – Tachikawa

DISTANCE: 5-6 KM | BEST ON WEEKDAYS

Built to commemorate the 50th anniversary of the reign of Emperor Showa, Showa Kinen spans over 160 hectares, making it the largest park in Tokyo. With this size comes the fact that it houses unrivaled variations of flowers and trees, so don't hold back visiting more than once, especially in different seasons. It's not just for lovers of nature and flowers too, but also the perfect spot for a casual afternoon bicycle ride.

Showa Kinen could be done on foot, but with the long distances involved and the ease of getting around on the dedicated cycle lanes, it's highly recommended to rent a bicycle. These can be rented after entering either the main entrance on the east side, or the Nishi-Tachikawa entrance (600 yen for three hours). Alongside the bicycle lanes are dedicated parking areas as well.

450 yen • 9:30am-5pm (until 4:30pm in winter and 6pm on summer weekends)

Starting and ending points

The nearest station is Nishi-Tachikawa (north exit), on the Ome Line, which has an entrance just outside. It'll take about 45 minutes to get here from Shinjuku Station in central Tokyo.

You'll probably need to change at Tachikawa Station, which is itself several minutes away from the main entrance on the east side of the park. Definitely enter via Tachikawa station in autumn, so as to see the **Ginkgo Promenade**.

Places of interest

Japanese Garden
Designed to condense all the main aspects of a traditional garden that you'd see across Japan, Showa Kinen's Japanese Garden ticks off all the boxes. The idea is that as you walk around the pond, you'll be able to enjoy ever-changing scenery, from stepping stones and a classical wooden bridge to bamboo fences and a tranquil waterfall. There's also a delightful little bonsai garden. It's a little extra to get in, but pop in if you have time.

1200 yen extra • Same opening times as park

Flower Hill
Poppies in spring, cosmos in autumn, and more throughout the year. The panoramic views from the top of the hill are spectacular.

There's also a small history museum, called **Komorebi Village**. Housed inside some Edo period mud buildings, visitors can see the tools of various trades from the olden times, as well as learn a bit about how Japanese people lived back then.

Flower Gardens
These gardens have a western edge to them, with a grand lawn in the middle reminiscent of many parks in Europe. The big draw here is the tulip garden, created by the former director of Keukenhof Gardens in the Netherlands. The best time for tulips is late March to mid-April.

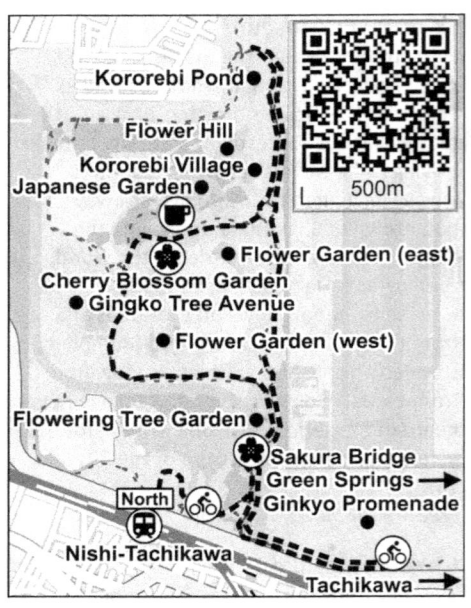

Inside Showa Kinen Park

Autumn leaves

Usually best in November, the golden leaves will be the first thing to catch your eyes at the **Ginkgo Promenade**. Located as you approach the main gate (Tachikawaguchi), the promenade has more than 100 ginkgo trees lined up in two rows on each side of an expansive waterway.

The other main spot for autumn leaves is **Gingko Tree Avenue**, which was left from the days when the site used to be a US military base. This corridor of gingko trees, or 'golden tunnel' as they call it in Japan, is the busiest spot in this season. Running about 300 meters, you'll need to get off your bicycles to take it in, but the dynamic views are rather breathtaking.

Also note that during this season the park will be open late, with the above areas and the Japanese Garden lit up for visitors, so definitely start your bicycle ride in the late afternoon to enjoy this. Only the Nishi-Tachikawa gate will be usable in the evenings.

Cherry blossoms

There are around 1500 cherry blossom trees that are usually in bloom from late March to early April.

As you make your way around there are some main sakura spots. The **Cherry Blossom Garden**, on the park's northern end, has some grand trees with huge branches stretching down to eye level, and combined with the daffodil fields you can really pack lots into your holiday pics. Other top cherry blossom spots include the **Sakura Bridge**, with a river below full of pink and white petals. The **Flowing Tree Garden** to the north side of the bridge also has plum trees, old cherry orchards and plenty of other flowery delights. There are plenty of picnic spots if you want to bring in a bento or supermarket sushi and relax under the cherry blossoms.

Recommended cafe

Head to Kanfu-tei in the Japanese Garden for an invigorating Japanese cafe experience. Patrons can enjoy a rich green tea with an old-fashioned sweet, while gazing out over the traditional pond and garden. It doesn't get more Japanese than this.
Tea and sweets sets 610 yen • 10am-4pm (until 3:30pm in winter)

Recommended meal spot

Green Springs is Tachikawa's hippest new area to hang out for a meal, and a drink or two. Inside, **Rojiura Curry** should be a safe selection for a meal. It specializes in upmarket Japanese soup curry, with a menu rich in vegetables. There's a massive selection of additional toppings, so you can really customize to your tastes.
Meals around 1500 yen • 11am-9:30pm

Bonsai plants at the Japanese Garden

Combine with...

It takes a while to get here, so why not combine this cycling ride with Fussa (p66), an American style town up the JR Chuo Line.

Little America – Fussa

DISTANCE: 3.5 KM | BEST ON WEEKENDS AND NATIONAL HOLIDAYS

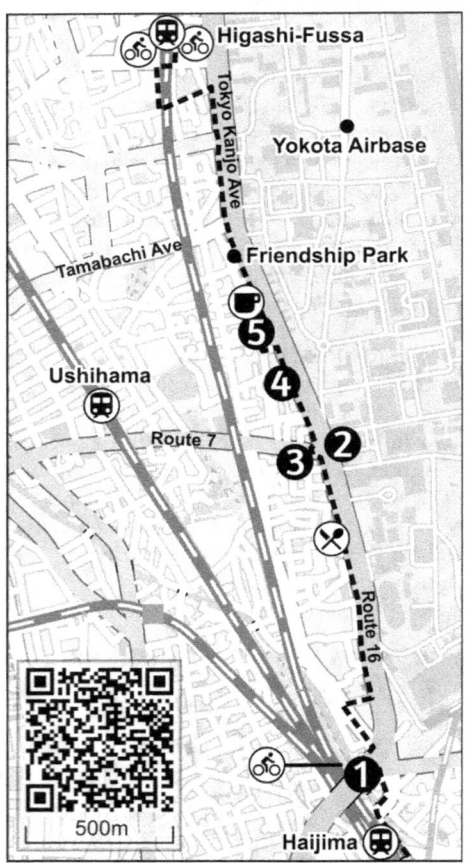

Places of interest

1) Nikko Bridge
The oldest brick-built arch bridge in the whole country, built in 1891. The original red bricks can still be seen as you look under it.

2) Yokota Base Gate No. 5
Grab a selfie at the huge U.S. Air Force sign. Sadly we aren't usually allowed in, but you'll be able to have a peek through the gates.

3) Tom Sawyer Workshop
This nutty store, run by an equally nutty owner who became a bit of a TV star for a while, is packed with his crazy yet imaginative homemade goods, as well as miscellaneous goods he has collected from events in Tokyo. *9:30am-5pm*

4) Big Mama
Antiques store, mainly selling American golden age items from the 50s and 60s. Loads of fun items, from tableware to retro posters. *11am-5pm • Closed on Thursday*

5) Base Side street
The road alongside the base is amazing for window shopping, and this hotspot is where Japanese come to experience the atmosphere of America. The **Fussa American House**, a building that was used by soldiers in the past, allows visitors to take a tour of a 1950s interior and gallery (free, 10am-7pm).

After the surrender of Japan in 1945, the American army established Yokota Air Base in Fussa. These days it houses both the United States Air Force as well as the Japanese air defense headquarters, with around 14,000 personnel. The surrounding area has very much been influenced by American culture, so it's quite a unique exclave to visit.

Starting and ending points

Start at Haijima Station (East Exit), which is accessed from Shinjuku in central Tokyo via the Chuo and Ome lines in about an hour. The route then ends at Higashi-Fussa, one station up on the Hachiko Line.

A festival near the American House

Recommended cafe
Blue Seal, AKA the Big Dip, is a favorite with base residents. The Okinawan ice cream shop has a bunch of wild flavors, from royal milk to tropical marble, plus normal flavors!
From 400 yen • 11am-10pm

Recommended meal spot
Take in the retro 50s decor at Demode Diner, a roadside diner where you can enjoy real American burgers, fried chicken and shakes.
Meals 1200-2000 yen • 11:30am-9:30pm

Cycling Shakujii River – Oji to Itabashi
DISTANCE: FROM 6 KM | BEST ON BICYCLE

Stretching from Sumida River, Shakujii is a pristine stretch of river crossing several wards, hidden away from the crowds downstream. It's a great cherry blossom route, but it's rather pleasant in summer and autumn too.

Outside the cherry blossom season, it might be best to cycle this long path. During the peak season, bicycles should be fine most of the way, apart from a few sakura spots. Another tip is to start super early, to avoid the slow day walkers.

Starting and ending points
Oji Station (Central Gate), on the JR Keihin-Tohoku Line, is a convenient place to begin. On the main route you'll reach Itabashihoncho, on the Toei Mita Line.

Places of interest

1) Oji
Oji is not known as a tourist spot, but has supermarkets and convenience stores to pop into before you head off. **Otonashi Water Park** (24h, free), which used to be an old river channel, makes for a peaceful start to your day. The nearby **Oji Shrine** (9am-5pm, free) is a 14th century site with a huge gingko tree.

2) Along Shakujii River
As this is a quiet residential area, the sights won't blow you away, but they make for nice stops along the way. First up, **Otonashi Sakura Green Park** (24h, free) has a neat wooden bridge suspended over traditional stone paths and streams. Not long afterwards is **Kongoji Temple** (24h, free), a little Buddhist temple known both for having a cemetery sheltered by numerous cherry blossom trees, as well as for Momiji leaves in autumn. Next door is **Otonashi Momiji Green Park** (24h, free), another beautiful spot for both seasons.

Continuing on you'll bump into **Yatsu Daikannon**. An 8.5 meter bronze statue of Buddhist deity Kannon, it is said to weigh five tons. It's quite odd to see such a thing in a residential area like this. There are also plenty of bridges along the way if you need to cross to avoid groups of people, or if you want to get that ultimate sakura shot.

3) Old Nakasendo Street
Modern yet understated shopping street, this is the place to see local residents doing everyday activities. This area was the first port town on the old Nakasendo Trail, which used to connect Edo (now Tokyo) to Kyoto. It was the last stop before samurai visited the shogun, and the first before setting off on the potentially dangerous trip to the south.

4) Extend to Toshimaen (extra 8 km)
The river extends much further west, so a worthwhile idea is to continue all the way to Toshimaen's Niwa-no-yu. All the usuals of a modern hot spring complex are here, such as a Japanese restaurant, several saunas and massage rooms. It has both a naked area, as well as a shared swimsuit area.
Around 2000 yen • 10am-11pm

When Tokyo really doesn't feel like a city – Machida

DISTANCE: 9 KM | BEST ON A BICYCLE

At first glance, Machida might seem to be outside Tokyo, but it's actually a large outcrop on the city's west side. While around Machida Station feels just like any other Tokyo concrete jungle, heading a few train stops away makes quite a difference.

Feeling at points like the suburbs, and at other times almost like the countryside, this area makes for a 100% non-touristy afternoon of cycling. I actually lived in this area for a year, so consider this to be a fully customized route from a local expert!

Starting and ending points

From Shinjuku Station in Tokyo, get on the Odakyu Line and make your way to Tsurukawa Station. A change at Shin-Yurigaoka may be required if you take an express train. Head out of the main exit to pick up your bicycles.

Around **Yakushiike Park**, at the end, there are a few bus stops (bus route no.55), that either head back to Tsurukawa (northbound) or to Machida Station (southbound). Bus departures are regular and IC cards or cash are accepted. If there are no bikes available at the beginning, you could easily do this route in reverse.

Places of interest

1) Tsurumi River

An always quiet stretch of river, resembling a canal much of the way. Passing through the suburbs on a flat path, it's an easy ride whatever the season. Stop off at **Beans Farm** (11am-6pm, from 400 yen, closed Mondays), a top rated cafe, if you need a break about halfway through.

2) Lotus Pond

Drop off your bikes and take a walk around the first section of **Yakushiike Park**. Also known as Hasuda, this botanical garden is beautiful any time of the year, but from late July to August the lotus flowers will be blooming.
Free • 6am-6pm

3) Shikisai no Mori

The main area of **Yakushiike Park**, and named as one of Japan's 100 Historical Parks. As well as the classics like sakura blossom trees, it has flowers for all the seasons. The bountiful nature attracts Machida people looking for relaxation time, without having to drive out to the actual countryside.

In the center is **Yakushi Pond**, which was used in pre-modern times to dam spring water for local agriculture. Surrounding it is the **Former Nagai Residence** and the **Former Ogino Residence**. The former is a farmhouse built in the 17th century, which was moved and restored at the park. Inside is a collection of old agricultural machines and tools. The latter is from the Edo period, and functioned both as a hospital and townhouse. Both are usually open to visitors.

The **Yakushi Chaya** tea store offers pleasant views over the pond and is known for its anmitsu, a simple Japanese dessert made using red bean paste, jelly and fruit. There are also a few seasonal gardens nearby, such as the **Peony Garden** (mid-April to May) and the **Dahlias Garden** (July to November).
Free • 24h

4) Fukuoji (Yakushido)
Peaceful little Buddhist temple up the northern hill. It contains the seated statue of Yakushi-yorai, the Buddha of healing and medicine, which is thought to have been made in the 11th or 12th century. The statue is not always open for viewing, but as the slightly hidden temple is a registered Tangible Cultural Property it's worth walking up to. There's also a 500-year-old ginkgo tree.
Free • 6am-6pm

5) Machida Squirrel Garden
Around 200 Taiwan squirrels have been left to roam around this garden, munching on the sunflower seeds that visitors can hand out. Squirrels aren't common in Japan like much of Europe, so people in Japan have to come to such a spot to see them for real. The little creatures are very much used to seeing people, and will run and climb all over you.
500 yen • 10am-4pm • Closed on Tuesdays (except national holidays)

6) Shikisai no Mori Western Garden
I was quite surprised to come across this garden on my first visit. While the previous spots seem like they haven't changed for centuries, the Western Garden is an almost brand new complex, and actually won a Good Design Award in 2020. As well as hilly lawns, workshops and observation deck, be sure not to miss the low-key store. This sells produce from community and co-operative farms in the Machida area, such as tofu, honey and fresh vegetables.
Free • 5am-10pm

Recommended cafes
Grab a light meal or drink at the easy to miss Sunmelt Coffee. Located in a backyard down a narrow alleyway in the suburbs, it does feel like a secret spot. Most popular is the grilled cheese sandwich.
Drinks from 500 yen • 10am-5:30pm • Closed on Mondays

Recommended meal spot
I'd recommended finishing at 44 APARTMENT Yakushiike, in the Western Garden. An airy, cozy restaurant overlooking the lawn, it uses the local produce that'll be found in the community store. Simple but hearty foods are served, like rice plates and hamburger sets.
Around 1000 yen • 8am-9:30pm

Fukuoji in Yakushiike Park

Tokyo side trips

Japan's biggest Chinatown – Yokohama

DISTANCE: 2.6 KM | BEST ON FOOT DUE TO CROWDS AND NARROW LANES

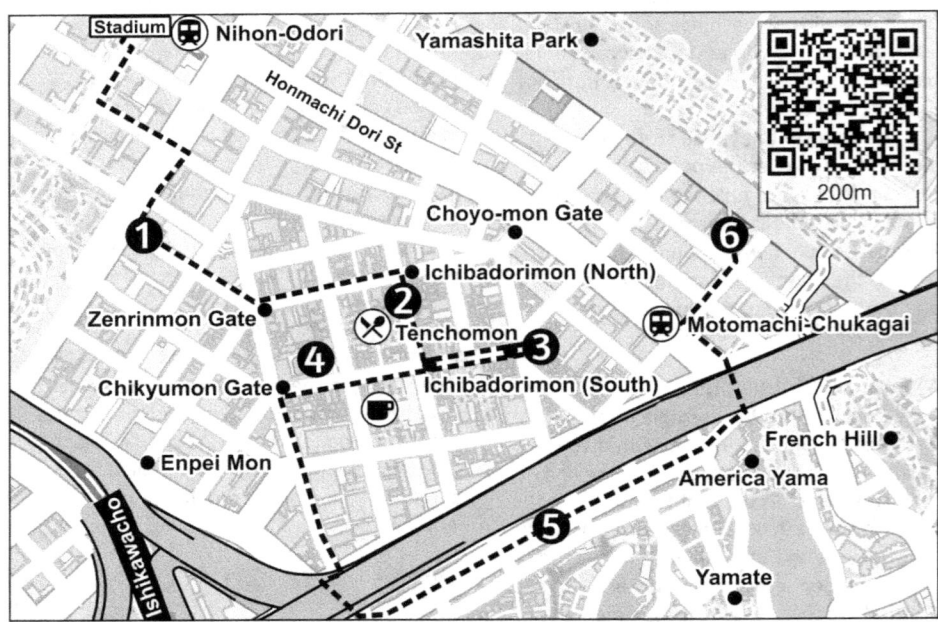

Several hundred Chinese shops, restaurants and snack stalls are packed into Chukagai, Yokohama's Chinatown. The history of the area dates back to 1859 when Yokohama's ports opened to Chinese merchants, with many then settling in this community. Nowadays it's a renowned tourist spot for domestic tourists, enthralled by a world of brightly colored signs and buildings.

Starting and ending points

From Shibuya in Tokyo, take the Tokyu Toyoko Line to Nihon-Odori and come out from the Stadium Exit. You'll end up near Motomachi-Chukagai, at the end of the line.

Places of interest

1) Genbumon Gate
There are four main gates, and five more dotted around the neighborhood, like Genbumon. Tradition is to enter Chinatown through one of the gates, with the main ones named after the four directions, also as per Chinese traditions. Each has had a guardian deity enshrined in it too, in accordance with Feng Shui. Just like the red torii gates at Japanese shrines, it is believed these gates, and their deities, protect the town.

Zenrimon Gate

2) Ichiba Dori Shopping Street

Street food should be at the top of your menu. Chinese steamed buns, known here as 'nikuman', are everywhere. Loaded with chopped pork, leeks and other greens, it's a must eat.

If you want something a little sweeter, try the red bean paste filled buns, which sometimes come in adorable panda-shaped buns. Shoronpo, small dumplings with hot juice inside, and yaki-guri, chestnuts roasted before your eyes, are also delicious. Many vendors offer free samples, so take your time to make your pick.

If you are interested in shopping, there are countless shops selling Chinese herbs, medicines and spices, plus many traditional tea shops.

3) Yokohama Daisekai

Now for something more over the top, and a little silly at times. Daisekai is an eight-story mega complex containing the biggest souvenir shop in Chinatown, the **Yokohama Chocolate Factory**, plus the comical **Trick Art Museum**.

At the chocolate factory you'll be able to view the tasty journey of chocolate creation as you watch the skilled chocolatiers through glass windows. Afterwards, you can of course scoff on some freshly made treats!
Entrance free • 9:30am-10pm

4) Kuan Ti Miao Temple

Confucian temple housing the deity Guan Yu, a legendary military general of the late Eastern Han Dynasty. The temple is a hallmark of Chinatown and is therefore decked out with dramatic ornamentation, such as dragons protruding from the roof and vibrant red color schemes. Staff, who speak English, are known to be particularly eager to answer questions and show tourists how to light the incense or pray at the altar.
Free • 9am-7pm

5) Motomachi Shopping Street

Cross over the river and you'll enter the very European looking Motomachi. It'll be a real contrast, lined up with jewelry, antique and furniture stores, in addition to a host of upmarket eateries and cafes. It'll be a bit pricey for some, but the architecture makes it a worthwhile walking spot.

6) Yokohama Marine Tower

Renovated in 2022, the Yokohama Marine Tower is certainly a neat spot for views over **Yokohama Bayside**. A top tip is to arrive in time for sunset, when you can see a clear silhouette of Mount Fuji. Night-time is also lovely, with views over all the dazzle below.
1000-1200 yen • 10am-10pm

Recommended cafes

Using tea imported from across China, Goku Tea House's cafe feels reminiscent of old Shanghai. You can also try popular Chinese sweets, such as the fluffy Chinese castella cake and desserts packed with tapioca, grass jelly and all sorts of other mysterious things!
Drink sets 600-1000 yen • 9:30am-7:30pm

Recommended meal spot

Try out a variety of Chinese food at Shichifuku, with a regular menu that offers a choice of around 130 items. I go for their dim sum course with 65 items, as this is their signature selection, and consistently spoken off as authentic by Chinese residents.
2000-3000 yen • 10:30am-10:30pm

Combine with...

You'll end up at Motomachi-Chukagai Station, from where the Yamate walk, in the next chapter, begins. If you're a really quick walker you might be able to do both in a day.

Yokohama's waterfront

Yokohama's foreign streets from years gone by – Yamate

DISTANCE: 3 KM | BEST FOR WALKING, AND NOT ON WEDNESDAYS

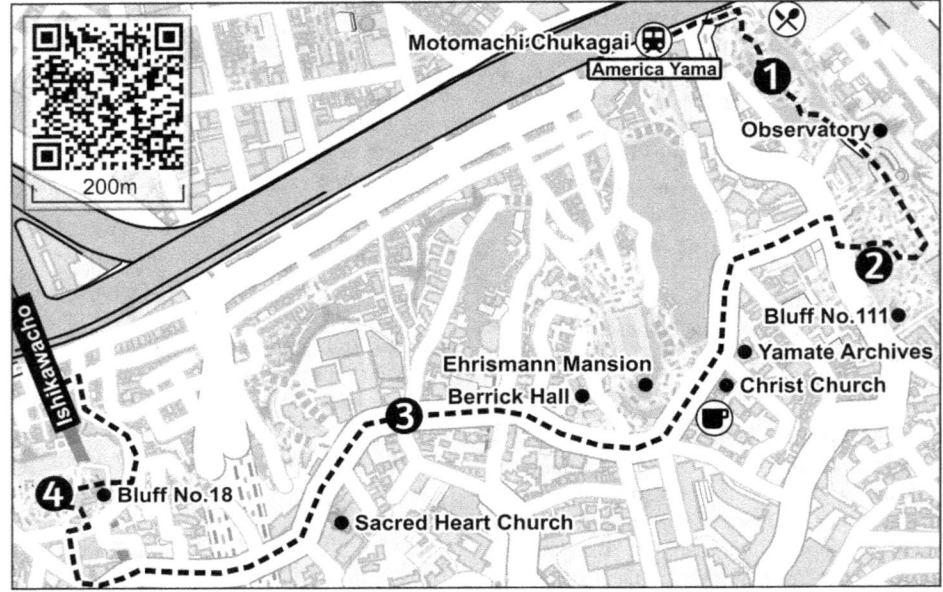

Up a hill on the southern side of Yokohama is Yamate, the main site in Kanto where western traders and diplomats flocked when, after centuries of isolation, the ports were opened to foreigners in 1853.

It soon became an incredibly prosperous area for business. As more foreigners arrived, the new locals started to build churches, homes and schools. Many of these colonial buildings were built in a style reminiscent of the immigrants' origin countries, setting Yamate apart from anywhere else in Kanto.

Starting and ending points

From Shibuya, take the Tokyu Toyoko Line to Motomachi-Chukagai and head out of the America Yama Park Exit. The path then ends at Ishikawacho, from where you can take a train to Tokyo, via Yokohama Station.

Places of interest

1) French Hill Park

Named so because the French consulate once stood here, this park was built after the Great Kanto Earthquake destroyed the complex. The remains of some old buildings and a windmill, which pumped water up to the consulate, have been kept for visitors to explore as they walk up.

Once at the top, the Harbor View Park Observatory offers views over the Minato Mirai 21 district on the waterfront, with Yokohama Bay Bridge behind it. It's a steep climb up, but well worth it for the scenery.
Free • 24h

2) British House

The British consular residence from 1937, this building is located on the edge of an English rose garden, which is in full bloom from April to June. Inside, the guest rooms, dining rooms and sun porch feel like they have come straight out of a colonial-period drama, plus there's also a wine cellar in the basement.

The next door Bluff No.111 is a Spanish-style building. It was originally the home of Mr. Ruffin, an American who lived in Japan for 15 years in the early 20th century.
Free • 9:30am-5pm • Closed on Wednesdays

One of the Bluffs on Hondori Street

3) Yamate Hondori Street

The main line of historical buildings can be discovered around Motomachi Park, on this main street. First up is the **Yamate Archives Museum** (11am-4pm, closed on Mondays, free). The only wooden Western style building that hasn't been moved, reconstructed or rebuilt, it houses interesting displays related to Yamate. Definitely come in here if you want to get more in-depth with this history. Just be mindful of the creaking floors and hallways!

Further up, the **Yokohama Christ Church** (times vary, free) looks like it was teleported here from the British countryside. It was actually originally constructed using Glasgow red bricks, carried over as ballast on steamships arriving from Britain. It was leveled by the Great Kanto Earthquake, before being rebuilt for the local English speaking community to use to this day.

Another highlight for many is the **Ehrismann Mansion** (9:30am-5pm, closed on Wednesdays, free). It was once owned by the Swiss manager of a silk trading company's Yokohama branch, which was one of the first European companies established in Japan. It was designed by Antonin Raymond, a Czech architectural pioneer at the time.

Finally, **Berrick Hall** (9:30-5pm, free) was lived in by English tradesman B.R. Berrick, and then used as a dormitory for St. Joseph International School. It's considered one of the greatest western-style structures in Japan.

It's not really necessary to visit all the western buildings here, so have a look from outside and see which takes your fancy.

4) Yamate Italian Garden

The location of the Italian consulate from 1880 to 1886, this peaceful garden stands atop a hill with sweeping views over Yokohama Bay Bridge and the rest of Yokohama. Affectionately named 'Mount Italy' by locals, it has been designed to imitate the styles often seen back in Italy.

Also onsite are the restored **Bluff No.18** and **Diplomat's House**. The residence of an Australian trader, this French-style Bluff was then used as a parish house of the Catholic Church. The other building was the residence of a Japanese diplomat in the Meiji government, and was designated a National Important Cultural Property. Both feature stately rooms with period furniture and are open for visitors to take a peek around.
Free • 9:30am-5pm

Recommended cafes

In the predictably elegant Bluff No.89-6 is Enokitei. Serving coffees, English sandwiches and afternoon tea in a terrace garden, it'll make you feel that little bit like the diplomats and rich traders of the past.
Snacks around 800 yen, drinks around 600 yen • 12pm-5:30pm (until 6pm on weekends)

Recommended meal spot

If you are tired of little Japanese burgers, have a hankering for a pulled pork sandwich or are missing a decent pizza, the American House Diner is the place to come. It's where the local foreign residents come, too.
Meals from around 1000 yen • 11am-10pm

Yamate Italian Garden

Hiking the mysterious Takinoo Path – Nikko
DISTANCE: 5 KM | CASUAL HIKING EXPERIENCE

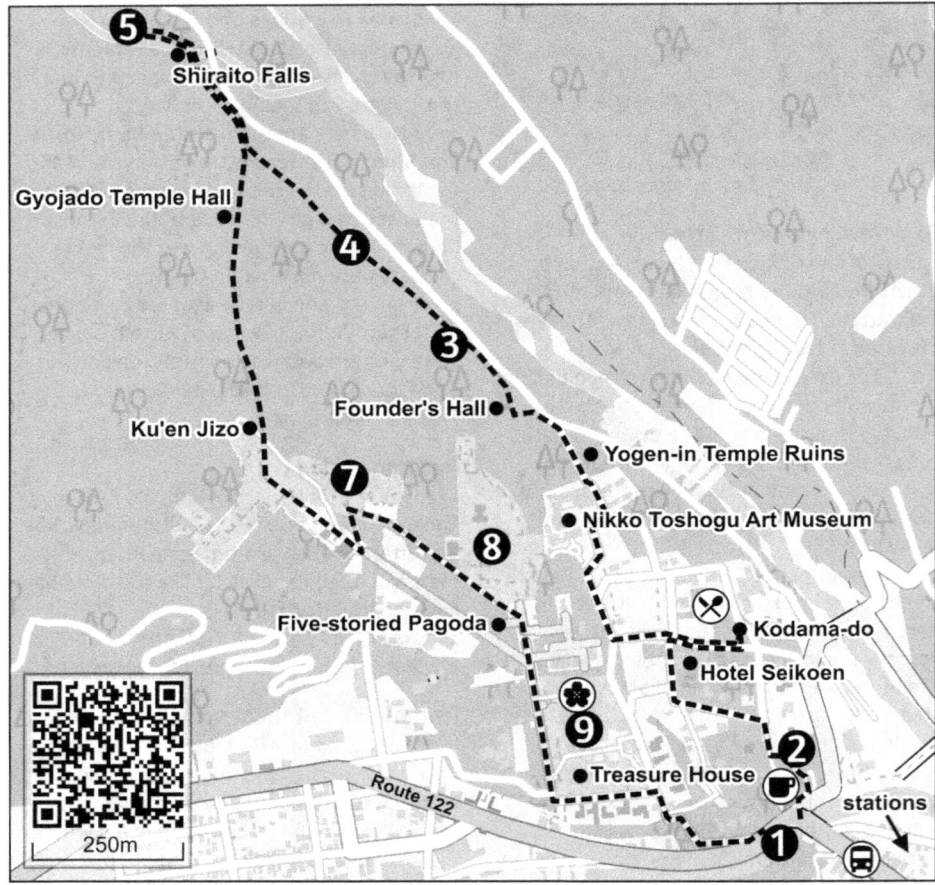

Nikko, one of the most popular weekend trips from Tokyo, is home to a smorgasbord of World Heritage shrines and temples. Starting at the famous red Shinkyo Bridge, Nikko's Takinoo Path takes walkers up and around famous tourist sites like Toshogu Shrine and Futarasan Temple. Rather than just heading straight into these busy tourist spots though, the route goes into a pristine forest course that takes you to off-the-beaten-track shrines and temples. Many of these are also World Heritage sites, but as they require a bit of a hike they unfortunately get missed by most day-trippers from Tokyo.

Starting and ending points

First you'll need to get to Tobu-Nikko Station from Asakusa in Tokyo. It takes about two hours, and it's recommended to get a Tobu Nikko pass, which includes a return on the trains plus unlimited use of the buses. Purchase at tobu.co.jp. If you have a Japan Rail Pass, head to Utsunomiya on the Shinkansen and transfer for a train to Nikko. Once in Nikko, take a local bus to the Shinkyo bus stop.

Places of interest

1) Shinkyo Bridge
One of Nikko's many iconic sites that must be featured on countless postcards. It's actually ranked as one of the three most beautiful in Japan.

Legend has it that a priest named Shodo Shonin was trying to cross the river, and was aided by a gigantic god who created a rainbow-colored bridge. Shonin went on to found many of the local shrines and temples in Nikko, and as the Takinoo Path traces a route he often used, you'll see his name mentioned frequently in the historical information signs featured at most sites. Note that you don't have to cross Shinkyo Bridge.
500 yen (to cross bridge) • 8:30am-4pm

2) Hongu Shrine
Our first World Heritage spot. One of the oldest structures in Nikko, Hongu is considered the birthplace of what eventually became Futarasan, a more famous shrine you'll encounter later. Visitors will also come across a three-storied pagoda and a simple Shinto hall enshrining the Goddess of Mercy. I was the only one here the last time I visited.
Free • 24h

3) Kannon-do (San-no-Miya)
A little further up we reach Kaizan-do and Kannon-do to its side. It may seem a bit weird to see a Shinto gate in front of a Buddhist temple, but this was built in a time when the practices and religions were often combined.

Venturing around the back you'll see six stone figures, which are Buddhist guardian deities. Other features include the Ying and Yang rocks, with a narrow rock representing the man, and the shorter, wider one representing a woman. Japanese people come here to pray for a safe childbirth.
Free • 24h

4) Kitano Shrine
It's mainly moss-lined stone paths from here, past old cedar trees, without a vending machine in sight. There are loads of random little shrines, halls and stone figures along the way. Kitano Shrine houses a scholar from the Heian period, as the God of Study.

A little further up you'll pass the Dai-Shoben Kinzei monument. It used to be a notice telling past visitors not to relieve themselves around here, as it's a holy place!
Free • 24h

5) Takinoo Shrine
The halfway point of the hike, Takinoo Shrine is a World Heritage site, just like the more famous shrines and temples in Nikko, so you'll probably be amazed as to why there are so few people here. There are many things dotted around, such as sacred rock that answers prayers for safe births, waters that were said to produce some of the most delicious sake, and a luck testing gate too. If you manage to throw a stone through the gap at the top of this torii gate you get good luck, so give it a try if you can.
Free • 24h

Kaizan-do and Kannon-do

7) Futarasan Shrine
The first of the Nikko biggies. Futarasan is dedicated to the deity of Mount Futarasan, a nearby mountain that has long been a place of worship for locals. Inside this World Heritage site are sweeping 'irimoya' Chinese roofs, lush gardens and two samurai swords that became official National Treasures.
300 yen • 8am-5pm

8) Toshogu Shrine
This one enshrines Tokugawa Ieyasu, Japan's most famous samurai. Toshogu takes things up a notch with a magnificent five-story pagoda and Yomeimon Gate, covered in more than 500 intricate carvings of elders and

mythical beasts. Be sure to check out the vibrant wood carvings, such as the 'sleeping cats', an elephant said to have been made by an artist who had never seen one, and of course the world-famous 'three wise monkeys'.
1300 yen • 8am-5pm

9) Rinnoji Temple
Nikko's most important Buddhist temple is also full to the brim with elaborate carvings and more colorful structures than you would find at standard Japanese temples. Inside, Sanbutsudo Hall contains gold statues several meters high, and there is also a treasure hall housing more statues of Buddha.
400-900 yen • 8am-4pm

Recommended cafe
Hongu Cafe is a cozy lodge under the towering trees of Hongu Shrine. The menu focuses on sweets using traditional Japanese ingredients like matcha and azuki beans.
Drinks from 500 yen, Japanese sweets from 550 yen • 10am-5pm • Closed on Thursdays

Recommended meal spot
Dine like a Meiji era aristocrat at Meiji No Yakata. Originally constructed as a Western style cottage for an American merchant, the building now houses this lovely restaurant, offering Western dishes that have been altered for Japanese tastes.
Meals usually 1800-3000 yen • 11am-7:30pm

Exploring Kamakura by bicycle – Kamakura
DISTANCE: 9 KM | BEST ON WEEKDAYS

Kamakura is an ancient city blessed with magnificent temples, a beautiful coastline and beach upon beach to chill out on. This popular Tokyo day trip has to be done at least once by any Japan travel aficionado.

While the majority of travelers to Kamakura explore the main spots via the tram or train, it does mean that some of these hotspots become quite overcrowded at times. This cycle ride hits up the must-see destinations, yet gives plenty of breaks in-between, via the comparatively quiet seaside.

Starting and ending points
The best station to start from is Enoshima, on the Enoshima Electric Railway, where there are several bicycle hire outlets. You'll eventually reach Kamakura Station, which has frequent departures to Tokyo and Yokohama.

Places of interest

1) Ryuko-ji
Concealed away from the tourist trails is this rather unknown gem, with a minimalist, unpainted wooden gate. It's the only classically built wooden building of its type in the prefecture.

Be sure to include the short hike to the top of the hill. There are lots of little statues and ornaments as you head up, and at the summit is **Bussha Ritou**, an impressive statue and prayer tower brought over from India.
Free • 9:30am-3:30pm

2) Manpuku-ji Temple
Another religious site that too many tourists have never even heard of. While Manpuku-ji is on the small side, the inside is quite appealing. It was the place where warrior Minamoto Yoshitsune lodged, the man that rumors say escaped to China, becoming what some believe was Genghis Khan. The temple has capitalized on this rumor, and houses some interesting samurai gear and ancient scrolls.
200 yen • 9am-5pm

Big Buddha

3) Cape Inamuragasaki
This is where Japan's surfing history began, with many professionals living in the area and surfers coming from all over Japan to experience the waves. The scenic cape is also a perfect rest spot on your cycling ride, being at about the halfway point.

While probably best to come back to after your cycling ride, the cape also has a hot spring, **Inamuragasaki Onsen** (9am-9pm, 1500 yen). As well as having English instructions on how to use a hot spring, it's also known to be tattoo-friendly, with many other hot springs in Japan forbidding those with tattoos from entering.

4) Hasedera Temple
This 8th-century temple houses the statue of Kannon, the Buddhist goddess of mercy, which is believed to be the largest wooden statue in Japan. The temple lies on a forested hill, with amazing views as you gaze over the city. It does get busy, but Hasedera is still a must see.

The story goes that a monk named Tokudo Shonin commissioned two statues to be made from the same tree, with one being taken to Hasedera Temple in Nara, and the other thrown into the sea. The other statue unexpectedly washed up in Kamakura years later though, so Kamakura's Hasedera was built to enshrine it.
400 yen • 8am-5pm

5) Kotoku-in
Say hello to the big Buddha himself at the monumental symbol of Kamakura. Also known as the Kamakura Daibutsu, the 11.4 meter bronze statue was originally built in 1252 and is the second tallest in Japan. It's records galore in Kamakura!
300 yen (plus 50 yen to enter the Buddha statue) • 8am-5:30pm (until 5pm in winter)

6) Onari Street
Compared to Komachi Street on the east side of Kamakura Station, Onari doesn't get much press. It's a more laid back spot for craft stores, cake shops and clothing boutiques, and while it doesn't completely escape the crowds it still feels like a bit of an escape from them.

Along the way you'll sense the wonderful aroma of the **Chocolate Bank** (8am-5:30pm). Predictably located in the building of a former bank, this posh shop is the place to come for fancy chocolate bars, chocolate gateau and cacao tea.

Kibiya Bakery (10am-5pm, closed Wednesdays) is another place to treat yourself at the end of your cycling ride, just in a much healthier way. The artisan bakery really is a cut above the rest in Japan, plus you can complement the bread with a nice glass of wine and cheese board.

Recommended cafe
Grab yourself an Acai smoothie, Hawaiian pancake or just a 'Bullet Coffee' at The Sunrise Shack. This surfers cafe overlooks the beach and sea.
Drinks from 500 yen, snacks from 400 yen • 7am-6pm (until 6:30pm on weekends)

Recommended meal spot
If you want to try an everyday Japanese bento for a reasonable price, check out Hotto Motto near Enoshima Station (9am-10pm, from 500 yen). Gyudon, Japanese curry and stir-fried veggies; there should be something for anyone that likes rice.

If you're looking for a sit-down experience along the way, neighborhood favorite Sangosho Moana Makai has some wholesome Katsu curries (10:30am-8pm, closed Tuesdays, around 1500 yen).

Kamakura's island of power spots – Enoshima

DISTANCE: 4 KM | TRY TO AVOID WEEKENDS AND NATIONAL HOLIDAYS

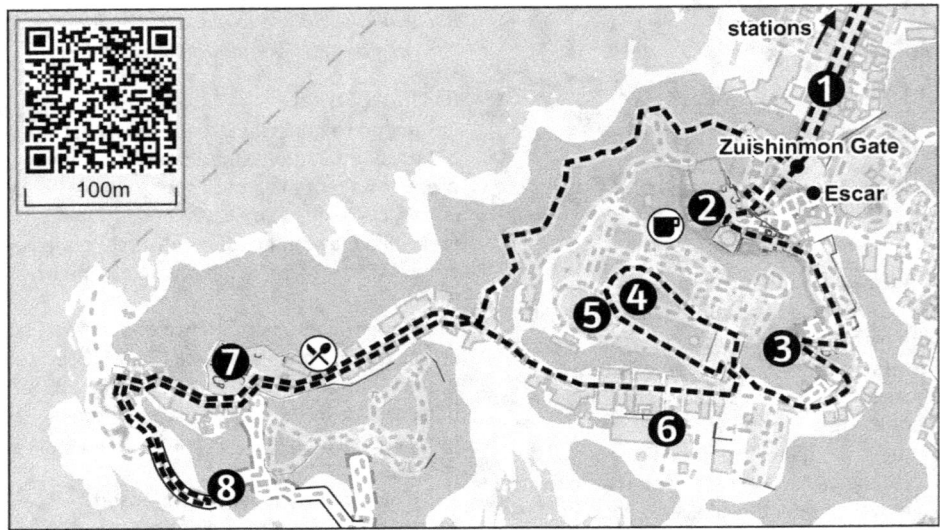

Enoshima is one of the most popular religious islands in Japan, and another essential day trip from Tokyo. It features a close-knit cluster of temples, statues and other spiritual structures, along with an observation tower and bit of hiking (or elevator if that's not your cup of tea).

Save some money by considering the Enoshima One Day Pass (1100 yen). Available from tourist information centers and the escalator booth, it includes access to the Sea Candle, Samuel Cooking Garden, Iwaya Cave and the Enoshima Escar.

Hiking up Zuishinmon Gate

Starting and ending points

The walk loops from either Katase-Enoshima (Odakyu Enoshima Line) or Enoshima (Enoshima Electric Railway) stations. It takes just over an hour from Tokyo to get here.

Places of interest

1) Benzaiten Nakamise Street

Head over **Benten Bridge**, and under the **Bronze Torii Gate**. With names of donors dating back to 1603 carved into the columns, you'll get a real sense of how for centuries it has been highly regarded as a religious site. The street itself has not been widened or seemingly changed much since these times, and remains a bustling line of souvenir shops and Japanese inns.

Once you get to the end, you have a choice of hiking up the stone stairs, or taking the rather convenient **Enoshima Escar** escalator up (8:50am-7:05pm, 360 yen). It takes about 20 minutes to climb the stairs on foot, and while steep, isn't too difficult for most.

2) Enoshima Shrine - Hetsunomiya

Enoshima Shrine is actually split up into three main parts, all of which you'll pass on this walk. It was fittingly built to worship the deities of fishing and tea transport, with each part dedicated to a different goddess of the sea. Your first port of call, Hetsunomiya, houses a majestic prayer hall.
Free • 8:30am-5pm

3) Enoshima Shrine - Nakatsunomiya

Next up is Nakatsunomiya, founded in 853, and the oldest shrine on the island. This was frequented by many Kabuki actors during the Edo period, as it also contains deities to music and the arts. These actors donated stone lanterns to the shrine, and around 150 carvings are now on display.
Free • 8:30am-5pm

4) Samuel Cocking Garden

A botanical garden established by an English merchant during the Meiji period, it mixes European and Japanese styles to create quite an exotic feel. South Pacific flowers and other seasonal flora can be seen, which are also lit up at night in the winter.
500 yen • 9am-8pm

5) Enoshima Sea Candle

A lighthouse observation tower in the center of the island, offering fully panoramic views from 110 meters above sea level. On clear days you'll get postcard-worthy views of Mount Fuji.

If coming in early April or September, you might be lucky enough to see the 'Diamond Fuji', an optical phenomenon where the sun sets just behind Mount Fuji, creating a diamond-like glow.
500 yen • 9am-8pm

6) Enoshima Daishi

Buddhist temple with two remarkable six-meter high statues of Fudomyo at its entrance. The protector of Buddhism, the rather intimidating appearance is meant to scare off potential intruders.

But tourists are more than welcome, and inside you'll be welcomed by a mixture of Chinese embroideries, with modern and Japanese architecture. Much of the temple is actually not that old, with the official founding in only 1993, so it's a little different from your standard neighborhood temple.
Free • 24h

7) Enoshima Shrine - Okutsumiya

The last part of Enoshima Shrine is known for its mural of a turtle looking out in all eight directions, a masterpiece by the Edo artist Sakai Hoitsu.
Free • 8:30am-5pm

8) Iwaya Caves

Carved out by centuries of tidal erosion, the Iwaya caves have long been a sacred area for Buddhists. You'll get to learn much about Enoshima's history from the exhibition inside, as well as from the ukiyo-e art of the island.
500 yen • 9am-5pm

Recommended cafe

Umitama Do is a cool little cafe selling sweets and cakes made with ingredients from Fujisawa, where Enoshima is located.
Drinks from 500 yen, snacks from 400 yen • 11am-7pm

Recommended meal spot

Relax at Tousha with a teishoku meal, sets served with rice, miso soup and Japanese pickles. Here they come with locally caught seafood and seasonal vegetables.
Meals usually 1500-2000 yen • 11:30am-6pm

Combine with...

Afterwards, why not cycle around Kamakura (p76), therefore hitting up most of the main spots in the Kamakura and Enoshima area in one swoop?

Nakatsunomiya

Exploring Kanto's top resort town by bicycle – Karuizawa
DISTANCE: 10 KM | AVOID VISITING ON NATIONAL HOLIDAYS

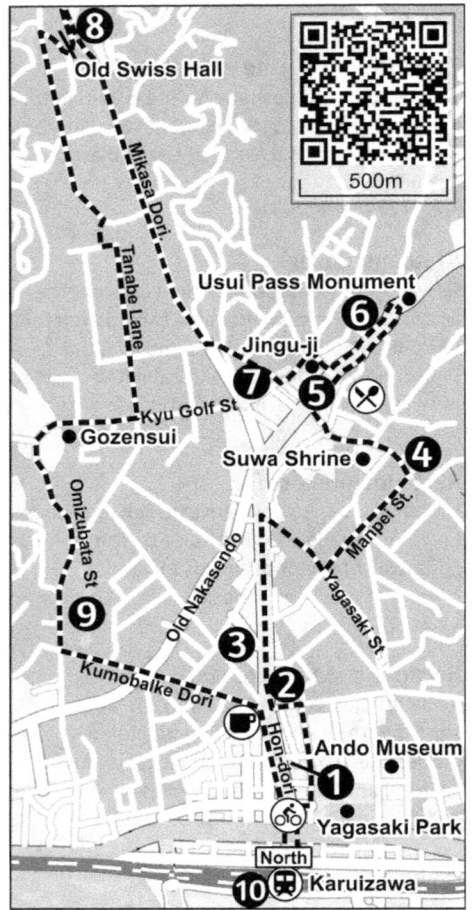

Karuizawa has been a favorite retreat for wealthy Tokyoites since the 19th century, particularly foreign expats looking for a spot to escape the summer heat of the capital. As bustling a tourist town as you'll find in Japan, it has countless shopping and dining opportunities and is surrounded by luscious woodlands. Visiting for a day or two is easy, and cheap if you have a train pass.

Starting and ending points

Karuizawa Station is located on the Nagano Shinkansen, with frequent departures from Tokyo (1 hour), as well as highway bus lines. You'll find several bicycle rental shops, with one near the north exit and more up the main road north of here. It's usually 500-600 yen for a regular bicycle and around 1000 for an electric-assisted one.

Places of interest

1) Petit Museum (Wild Flower Museum)
As the name suggests, this museum won't take too much time, but many will take pleasure in seeing the works by Ishikawa Koichi, a well-known creator of watercolor sketches and oil paintings, mainly of the flora around Karuizawa.
Free • 10am-5pm • Closed on Tuesdays

2) Karuizawa New Art Museum
Contemporary art museum with a mission to put Japanese artwork on the global stage, in particular post-war era artists. It's managed to acquire art that has gained lots of international acclaim, such as the Gutai Art Collective, so it's a must-see for art fans. Check out what's on when you're visiting at knam.jp/en, as special exhibitions can range from cute and crazy to somber, and what's on might affect if you decide to visit.
2000 yen • 10am-5pm • Closed on Mondays

3) Wakita Museum of Art
Small museum showing off oil paintings, drawings and prints by Kazu Wakita. Wakita lived in Germany in the 1920s and during the war, where he took on a western style. His art mainly focuses on birds, flowers and children, giving a sense of warmth and purity.
200 yen • 10am-5pm

4) Manpei Hotel
Back in the day this was John Lennon and Yoko Ono's preferred place to stay when visiting Karuizawa. The bar has become a watering hole for a bunch of other celebrities too, so Japanese people love to have a peek

inside this hotel. If you would like to try the milk tea that Lennon always had, take a seat at **Cafe Terrace**.
Cafe sets from 2000 yen, drinks from 650 yen • Cafe open 10am-5pm

5) Old Karuizawa Ginza Street
The historic heart of the town, lined with an endless supply of posh boutiques, cafes and eateries. It runs along what was the old Nakasendo Trail, which you may have also traversed in Sugamo (p42) and Itabashi (p67).

6) Karuizawa Shaw Memorial Church
Built in 1895, this is Karuizawa's oldest church, being founded by Anglican minister Alexander Croft Shaw. He spread the word about this summer resort, helping to popularize it in the 19th century, after which many more churches were built. Nestled among forest trees, the small wooden church has stunning stained glass windows. You can also look inside a recreation of Shaw's villa.
Free • 9am-5pm

7) St. Paul's Catholic Church
Another symbol of Karuizawa, this is a beautiful little Catholic church featuring a steep, triangular roof.
Free • 9am-4pm

8) Historic Mikasa Hotel
One of the oldest standing European-style hotels in Japan, and where most will aim as their furthest bicycle trip destination. Designated as an important cultural property by the national government, if you're not staying here you can still join a tour inside.
Free • 9am-6pm (reopening summer 2025)

9) Kumoba Pond
Picturesque pond with a nearly mirror-like reflection of the trees around it. Whether it's the autumn leaves, cherry blossoms or a summer green, it's easily one of Karuizawa's best tourist spots.
Free • 24h

10) Karuizawa Prince Shopping Plaza
Prince Shopping Plaza is a sprawling mall with 250 outlet shops, plus a food court with a wide enough range to suit all tastes. It's one of the main destinations for weekend trippers to splash their cash, or you can just relax on the grassy lawn after an energetic bike ride.
9am-9pm

Recommended cafe
Run by a very friendly barista and staff, Natural Cafeína has become a must visit for many expats who visit Karuizawa on weekends, with a menu that emphasizes natural, healthy ingredients. Generously sized cakes and killer coffees; it really hits the spot.
Drinks 600-900 yen • 8am-5pm (closed on Tuesdays and Wednesdays)

Recommended meal spot
Cozied away in the forests behind Ginza Street is Suzu no Ne. Offering family favorites like curry and taco rice (think taco fillings but on Japanese rice), it'll be a neat pick-me-up during your bike ride.
Meals usually 1300-1500 yen • 9am-5pm

Combine with...
If you want to escape the crowds of Karuizawa and have a day free, check out the next chapter on Karuizawa's lost railway.

Old Karuizawa Ginza Street

Manpei Hotel

The lost railway – Karuizawa's Apt Road
DISTANCE: 7 KM | BEST IN AUTUMN

Before the Nagano Shinkansen line was built the Usui Pass was used to travel from Tokyo to Karuizawa by rail, and had been a major transportation route since the 19th century. Notoriously tricky for trains to pass, it had to use a track and pinion system to drag the trains along gradients of up to 66 degrees. Largely dismantled, what's left now is a nature trail that's rich in railway history, and largely devoid of all the tourists in Karuizawa.

Starting and ending points

Take a bus or taxi from Karuizawa Station, which is on the Nagano Shinkansen line, to the Kumanotaira Parking Lot (熊ノ平駐車場). Check at the information center in the station the day before, as the cheaper buses only operate on an infrequent schedule. The path up is across from the parking lot.

You'll end up at Yokokawa Station. From here you can take the train to Takasaki, which has connections to Karuizawa and Tokyo.

Places of interest

1) Former Kumanotaira Station
This now rusting station used to be where the water and coal was kept for the steam locomotives, before becoming a signal station in the 60s. The area seems like it has been frozen in time since the line's closure, with a small shrine for railway workers and a huge plaque commemorating its construction. From here, continue through the dozen or so brick train tunnels.

2) Megane Bridge
This arched brick bridge is the biggest of its kind in Japan. Constructed in 1892, it was used for several decades as a rail bridge. You'll approach from the top, at a height of 31 meters. The most popular spot to take photos is from the bottom though, which can be reached via a trail near the start of the bridge.

Megane Bridge

3) Usui Lake
This beautiful man-made lake is an excellent spot to take a break. If you have time, it's also possible to walk around Usui Lake too. The views are spectacular, especially when the fall leaves are out. Along the way there is a special spot to get Instagram photos in front of **Sakamoto Dam**, plus a mysterious mining tunnel. Note there are toilets here if you need them, and watch out for monkeys!

4) Toge No Yu
At about the halfway point is this modern hot spring. There are two public baths, one Japanese and one Western style. From the outdoor baths, including some 'one-person' ones, you'll be able to enjoy views of the mountains. Private baths for families are also available, as are massage chairs and tatami rooms to lie down in.
From 700 yen • 10am-9pm

5) Old Maruyama Substation
A former electric substation that has been designated by the Japanese government as an Important Cultural Property, with the outside

being restored to its early 20th century glory. While the public can't go inside, if you get close up to the windows you should be able to get a decent look inside.

6) Usui Sekisho Checkpoint
Before the train line was constructed, the Usui Pass was part of the Nakasendo, one of the five vital paths that connected Edo (now Tokyo) with its provinces during the Edo period. This checkpoint was created to guard the entrance into the Kanto region, and to crack down on robberies. While much of the complex has been demolished, the west gate and an associated shrine remain to this day.
Free • 24h

7) Usui Pass Railway Heritage Park
Loads of retro locomotives that were used on the line, many of which you can have a peek inside of. From time to time visitors can experience a ride on a mini locomotive train and an open-air carriage train, or even try driving an electric locomotive. The park is a worthwhile visit if you want to learn more about the history of the Usui Pass.
700 yen • 9am-4:30pm • Closed on Tuesdays

Recommended cafe
Just before you get to Usui Lake you'll see this cute mountain hut up on the left. Inside, Korobokkuri is a gift shop selling handicrafts made using local forest materials, plus there's a charming cafe called Mini Mini. Cakes and toast are also available.
Drinks 400-500 yen • 10:30am-6pm

Recommended meal spot
There's not much available on the trail. I would therefore recommend bringing food with you, such as from a convenience store in Karuizawa, or eating there before you start. Having said this, Toge No Yu does have a restaurant serving basic meals like soba noodles and curry rice. Not going to win any awards, but the location is very convenient and this is the hearty food you'll need after all that walking.
Meals 600-900 yen • 10am-5pm

One of the shrines along the railway tracks

Hachioji Castle Ruins – Hachioji (near Mount Takao)
DISTANCE: 4-6 KM | MODERATELY DIFFICULT HIKE, BEST ON WEEKENDS

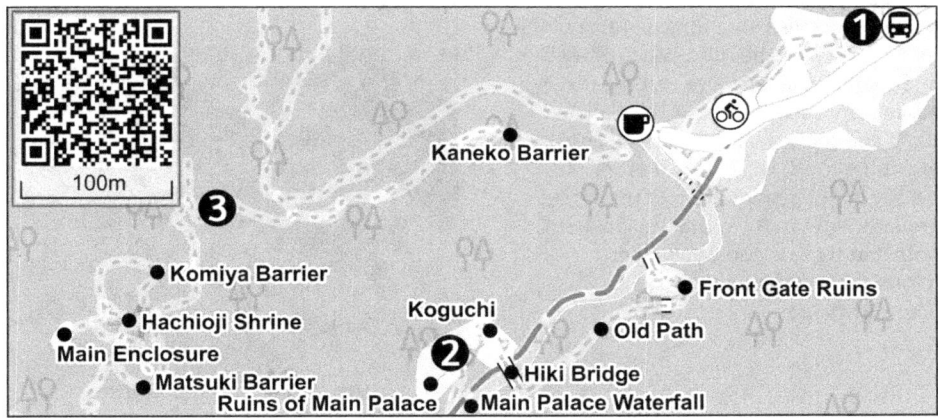

Hachioji Castle, once one of the main castles in the Kanto region, was built by a powerful feudal lord by the name of Hojo Ujiteru during the Warring States period (mid-15th century to the start of the 17th century). Unfortunately for him, though, in 1590 it was overwhelmed and burned down by Toyotomi Hideyoshi, a rival lord who was expanding rapidly across the country. As Hojo was also defending against a siege of nearby Odawara Castle (p89), Hachioji Castle was left with a skeleton defense that was unable to cope.

Excavation began on the site in the 1980s and uncovered the remains of the stone staircase and other buildings connected to the castle. These have since been restored, and the castle gate was reconstructed. While certainly not an A-list tourist spot, the castle remains, surrounded by dense forests and with plenty of hiking trails, makes for a nice day trip, especially for history buffs.

Starting and ending points

First make your way to Takao Station, about 45 minutes from Shinjuku on the Keio Line. On weekends and national holidays there is a bus service from the north exit. Take a Tokyo Bus to Reienmae/Hachiojijoseki Iriguchi and walk up the road. Alternatively, there are Hello Cycling stations outside the station and one in the car park near the grounds.

Places of interest

1) Hachioji Castle Guidance Hall

Make a quick visit here for a diorama of the mountain and castle ruins. Much of the information is in Japanese, but the text is easily scanned with Google Translate.

If you speak a bit of Japanese, enquire about the tours, which take visitors into usually out of bounds areas of the castle grounds. If no staff are available to assist, note that there is also a volunteer information center up the road too.
Free • 9am-5pm

2) Lower castle grounds

Start off by heading to the Main Palace ruins. You'll cross the river and pass a temple to join the **Old Path**, via the **Ruins of the Front Gate**. Not much of historical importance is viewable, but it's a wonderfully quiet forest path.

You'll eventually reach the reconstructed **Hiki Bridge**. Once the battle began it was destroyed in an attempt to prevent Hidetoshi's troops from crossing. Before this it was the main passageway into the castle.

Next you'll head up the faithfully restored, original stone stairs, to reach **Koguchi**, a recreation of the traditional wooden entrance. Inside there's a large open space containing the **Ruins of the Main Palace**. It used to feature the Lord's Palace, a guest house and Japanese garden, but was just left for centuries after the battle. The foundation stones of some buildings have been excavated, so you can get a bit of a feel for what once stood here. Some of the remains of pottery, and weapons of war, are on display at the Guidance Hall mentioned above.

Nearby is the **Main Palace Waterfall**. When the castle fell, many of the women, children and defeated defenders took their own lives here, with the water said to have turned red for three days and nights. It's much of the reason that the site was considered haunted, with few people visiting for the first three hundred years or so after the battle.
Free • 24h

Stone steps up to the front gate

Hiki Bridge

3) Hike up to Hachioji Shrine

While some might leave it here, it's highly recommended to hike up to **Hachioji Shrine**, as this is the location of the castle's **Main Enclosure**. As it's high up there isn't much flat ground, meaning that this part of the castle didn't have towers and gates that you'd expect in a Japanese castle. The unusually high location was thought to be a tactical advantage.

The shrine itself enshrines the guardian deity of Hachioji Castle. You'll see a few paths around the top, so spend a bit of time exploring the forest before heading back. I spotted a few little temple structures, and the views down below were superb.

Hiking up and down should take a few hours, and while steep at points it should be fine for most people. Most signage is in Japanese, but as there are always people around there is no need to worry about getting lost. The volunteers, in bright orange vests, are always eager to assist too.

Free • 24h (but rumored to be haunted, so a warning if you come at night!)

Recommended cafe

Joseki Tea House offers a few pick-me-ups like hot sweet potatoes, rice balls and shaved ice bowls. Yuzu teas, as well as coffees and green teas, are also served.

Drinks from 300 yen, snacks from 350 yen • 10am-4pm (closed Fridays and Mondays)

Recommended meal spot

After all that hiking, try out the local delicacy of Hachioji ramen. A simple soy sauce broth with butter and chopped onions, it can be found at highly rated Shunya-chan, a short walk from Takao Station.

Noodles from 750 yen • 6pm-11pm (closed Sundays and Mondays)

The path up to Hachioji Shrine

Hiking into the clouds – Mount Oyama

HIKING TIME: 4-5 HOURS (-1 HOUR IF USING CABLE CAR) | STEEP CLIMBS

Mount Oyama is a moderately popular hiking spot near Tokyo. The mountain is known for its rich nature, but much of the appeal comes from the fascinating sight of distant shrines and temples as you climb up, some of which you'll visit on this path. Many mountains in Japan have such structures up their paths, but Afuri Shrine is much bigger, as impressive as any you'll see in a city, and the scenery surrounding it makes it extra special. The traditional shopping street from the bus stop to the start of the trail is also a perfect photo and souvenir shopping spot. The area is also famous for its autumn leaves.

Starting and ending points

The easiest, and probably cheapest, way to get to Mount Oyama is to pick up a Tanzawa-Oyama Freepass from Shinjuku Station (Odakyu ticket area). The pass includes a return train ticket and buses to the mountains, with or without use of the cable car (1560 yen/2520 yen). Head to Isehara Station, about an hour on the train, then take a regularly departing bus to Mount Oyama. The final bus stop is from where this route begins and ends.

Places of interest

1) Koma Sando
The built-up section at the beginning of the route is lined with quaint souvenir shops, ryokans and tofu restaurants, giving the feeling of a tourist town away from over-commercialization. You can buy the actual 'Oyama Koma', traditional local toys that serve as good luck charms to their holders.

Along the way, you'll see brown signs on the stairs, which quiz you about the mountain as you hike up. Get out Google Translate and give yourself a mental as well as a physical challenge!

2a) Oyama Tozan Cable Car
Cut out about an hour or so of hiking by taking the cable car up. It departs every 20 minutes and takes visitors on a gentle, scenic 800-meter track up to near Oyama Afuri Shrine. As the hike up is quite steep, it's definitely recommended for most people.
Included with pass, or 650 yen • 9am-5pm

Walking up to Oyama Afuri Shrine

2b) Onna-zaka Path
There are two main routes up, Onna-zaka (woman's path) and Otoko-zaka (men's path). As the Onna-zaka path is less steep, it's the most popular hiking route up.

3) Oyama Temple
Locals come to have a go at 'kawarake-nage', a custom where you throw a small plate down the cliff, with the purpose of ridding yourself of bad luck and opening the opportunity to pray for your wishes to come true. Viewing the maple leaf trees here in Autumn is something special, with the red-leafed trees creating a tunnel as you approach the main gate.
Free • 24h

4) Oyama Afuri Shrine
I wasn't expecting a shrine like this when I first came to Mount Oyama. After being greeted with majestic stone stairs up to the torii gate, you'll get to see what is surely one of Japan's most beautiful mountain shrines.

The 'Afuri' in the name refers to the mountain's frequent heavy rain and clouds. Farmers have been coming here for more than 400 years to pray before the rain gods to help with their harvests. Have a look to the right of the main building and you'll see a long corridor to a natural spring water source, and many Shinto relics. It's usually possible to refill your water bottle here too. Afterwards, continue to the left of the shrine, via the mini **Sugawarasha Shrine**.
Free • 24h

5) Summit and Honsha
On a clear day you'll see as far as Mount Fuji, but if Mount Oyama is up to its normal tricks, it might start to get pretty foggy as you head up. It all adds to the atmosphere though. Be sure to bring a waterproof coat.

The path up is reasonably tough, but there are plenty of little disused Shinto buildings to rest at and check out along the way.

The summit's shrine, **Oyama Afuri Shrine Honsha**, has a very minimalistic plain wood design, with understated decorations and

color. It's a stark contrast from Oyama Afuri Shrine.
Free • 24h

6) Down via Otoko-zaka or cable car
If you're not taking the cable car down, take the Otoko-zaka path to spice things up a bit. Be really careful if it's been raining, as the rocks can get slippery.

Onna-zaka features what is known as the Seven Wonders, small religious spots along the way that are said to have magical properties. You'll also pass the Nijuno waterfall and an ancient cedar tree.

Recommended cafe
Just before you head up the main stairs to Oyama Afuri is the sweet little rest stop of Chaya Sakura-ya. Customers can sit on the rackety little tatami tables, and the menu here is just what you'll need for an energy boost. The udon and soba noodles seem to be the bestsellers, but they also sell dango sticks (sweet rice balls), sake and ice cream.
Food 600-800 yen • 9am-4pm

Recommended meal spot
Come to Kankiro or Mototaki, both at the end of Koma Sando, to enjoy Oyama Tofu. Made with the high-quality water flowing down the mountain streams, Oyama Tofu is a simple dish, usually without any meat or fish. Other restaurants down Koma Sando will offer their own variations too.
Meals usually 1800-3000 yen • 11am-7:30pm

Mount Nokogiri – Boso Peninsula, Chiba

DISTANCE: 2-3 KM WITH ROPEWAY (EASY), 7-9 KM WITHOUT (MODERATE)

One of the most beloved tourist spots in Chiba, the prefecture to the east of Tokyo. The hiking trails around the grounds of Nihon-ji Temple, at the top of Nokogiri, offering stunning vistas over Tokyo Bay and countless small, and very big, Buddhist monuments.

Starting and ending points

The hike takes place near Hama-Kanaya Station, which is 90 minutes from Tokyo Station on a JR special express train. It's well signposted from here, and there is also a tourist info center on the way if needed.

An interesting alternative is to take the Tokyo Wan Ferry (tokyowanferry.com), which crosses Tokyo Bay from the other side. It might make sense if you are staying in Yokohama or Kamakura the night before.

Places of interest

1a) Hike up Mount Nokogiri

If you would prefer to hike up and/or down, there are two main routes that start not far from the Mount Nokogiri Information Center, where you can pick up a seasonal trail map.

The Sharikimichi Trail is named after the 'shariki' laborers that used the path to transport stone blocks from the quarry up the mountain. Making the trip three times a day, the trail was carved from their carts going up and down. You'll also see the remains of rail tracks and pulleys that were used in later years.

The alternative Kanto Fureai No Michi Trail is a more direct route, but with steeper stairs, while Sharikimichi is more winding. Both take about an hour and lead you to the stone quarry ruins on the north side of the mountain.

1b) Mount Nokogiri Ropeway

The ropeway will cut out a significant amount of uphill hiking, so is perfect for beginner level hikers. The views as you go up are breathtaking, plus there also seems to be a friendly family of cats living at the top station! *One way 650 yen, round trip 1200 yen • 9am-5pm (until 5pm in winter)*

2) Jigoku Nozoki

Also known as the View of Hell, this is a lookout point protruding over the sharp cliff edges of Mount Nokogiri. You'll understand its name once you see the rather scary drop-off, and have an unnerving look down after. On a positive note though, the sunset views are world famous and you'll be able to see Mount Fuji to the west on most days.

The hanging rock observation platform

3) Hyakushaku Kannon

Directly carved into the wall of the sheer rock face is this 30-meter high Buddhist deity. Kannon, the Goddess of Mercy, was carved into the stone cliff in 1966, and is dedicated to those lost in war, accidents and of sickness.

4) Sengohyaku Rakan

There are 538 tiny statues of disciples spread around the temple grounds and in the various nooks and crannies along the spiraling paths. These 'Rakan' each have a unique facial expression and pose, so you could spend hours checking them all out. Some are quite humorous, chatting with their neighbors, while others look rather spooky and eerie.

As you walk around you'll see that many of them are headless, or have been desecrated in some way. This all occurred during an anti-Buddhist movement in the late 19th century, when Buddhist places of worship across Japan were attacked. It eventually led to Shinto being established as the state religion and the temporary outlawing of Buddhism. Thankfully, local authorities have been repairing much of the damage in recent years, and work is very much ongoing.

5) Kenkonzan Nihon-ji Temple

Nihon-ji claims to be the oldest place of worship in the Kanto region, being constructed 1300 years ago. This Soto Zen Buddhist temple is connected with the other sites in this chapter, making it a hugely extensive complex overall.

Note that you'll need to bring money for the entrance fee. There are no convenience stores for an ATM up here, or even any vending machines for a cool drink on a sunny day.

700 yen • 9am-10pm

6) The Big Stone Buddha

Let's ratchet things up a bit with this even more massive Buddhist monument, known in Japanese as Daibutsu. Another record here, it's the largest stone-carved Buddha in the country, and depicts the healing Buddha Yakushi, carved from 1780 to 1783. In one hand it holds a medicine flask; worshipers believe that if you were to bathe in the emerald of such a flask, your illness would be healed.

The wide-open area beside the Buddha has ample seating, so this is the spot to have a lunch bento.

Recommended meal spot

It'll be best to bring food with you, as there isn't anywhere for food in the temple complex. There is a 7-Eleven convenience store with a wide selection of bentos and sandwiches, between the station and ferry terminal (24h). JR Chiba Station, on the way from Tokyo, also has an excellent selection of food stalls inside its ticket gates.

But one restaurant/cafe that needs to be mentioned is **Sanga Soba & Coffee Stand** (11:30am-3pm, open Friday to Monday). Tempura made using locally caught fish, classic thin noodle plates and super friendly service; it's a surprise hit. Come here if arriving at lunchtime.

Daibutsu, AKA The Big Stone Buddha

Odawara Castle and the power of the Triforce – Odawara
DISTANCE: 2 KM | POSSIBLE TO WALK OR CYCLE

A link to the past not far from Tokyo, Odawara is an excellent stop off on the Tokaido Shinkansen if you want to see a traditional Japanese castle. Alternatively, visit here on the way to Izu Panorama Park (p91).

Starting and ending points

Odawara is about 30 minutes from Tokyo on the Shinkansen, or around 90 minutes if using standard JR or Odakyu line trains. You'll start and finish at the East Exit.

Places of interest

1) Tokiwa Kimon Samurai Centre
Rent some samurai clothes, or a classier kimono, and wander around the castle grounds like you're from the feudal times! There is also a small exhibition of real samurai armor and swords.
200 yen (cosplay from 500 yen) • 9:30am-5pm

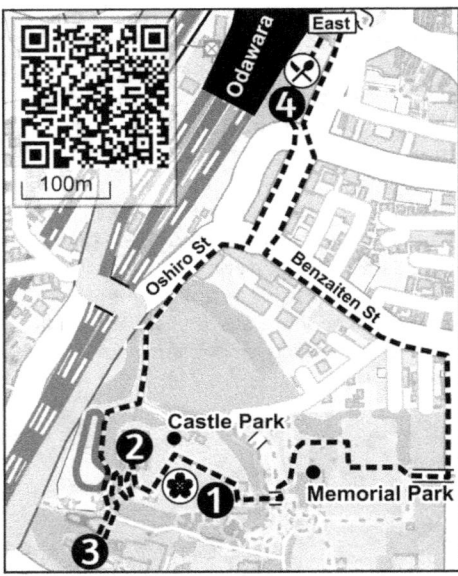

Odawara Castle

3) Hotoku Ninomiya Shrine
An unexpectedly calm retreat, with a koi pond, abundant greenery and minimalist, unpainted torii gates.
Free • 6am-6pm

4) Minaka Odawara
On the lower floors of this department store is an Edo-style mini town, looking like a row of small townhouses from days past. It's a convenient place to pick up some souvenirs, or try out some Edo-era snacks. There is also a footbath on the 14th floor, using hot spring water from Hakone, with ocean views.
Free • 10am-11pm (footbath until 8pm)

2) Odawara Castle
Odawara's must-see is this 15th century castle, famous for its flower filled park. From azaleas to plum trees, and of course cherry blossom trees, **Odawara Castle Park** is great any time of the year. It's also a very manageable walk from the station.

The castle itself was the base of the Hojo clan, who ruled over Odawara for more than 100 years, and is probably the best example of an Edo-period castle in the Kanto area. It's often overshadowed by others nationwide, but has fewer crowds, plus all the classic Japanese castle elements, such as a three-story castle tower, moats and main keep.
510 yen (with Samurai Centre 610 yen) • 9am-5pm

Recommended meal spot
Oden, a hotpot dish simmered in a dashi broth, is one of the city's specialities. The simply named Odawara Oden is the best place to try it out, with more than 40 kinds on offer.
100-500 yen per dish • 11:30am-9pm (closed on Tuesdays)

Minaka Odawara

Izu Panorama Park – Izu Peninsula

DISTANCE: 1-2 KM | LIGHT HIKING SPOT

Izu Panorama Park could be described as one of the most stylish mountains in Japan. Why? Well, it features a modern footbath at the top, plus a classy lounge and cafe with 360 views of Mount Fuji and the peninsula. It's therefore a perfect day trip for anyone, from families to single travelers. Once you are there everything is super easy.

Starting and ending points

It takes about 90 minutes to get here from Tokyo Station, if you use the Shinkansen and change at Mishima, but there are also cheaper trains that take about 2 hours. At Mishima, take the Izu-Hakone Line to Izu-Nagaoka. Finally, get on a bus bound for Nagaoka Onsen or Izu Mito Sea Paradise and get off at Izunokuni Shiyakushi-mae, a short walk from the start.

Places of interest

1) Izunokuni Panorama Park Ropeway
A highlight for many coming here, the almost 2km ropeway takes visitors up to an elevation of 452 meters. It's an impressive climb, with views gradually expanding to include the rural landscape of Izu-Nagaoka and Suruga Bay, and Mount Fuji coming into view as you reach the top.
2500 yen • 9am-5:30pm (until 5pm in winter)

2) Katsuragi Shrine
Located in the area at the top of the ropeway, called the **Ao Terrace**, Katsuragi was founded in the Heian period (794-1185) and contains a deity that wards off evil. Nearby is **Hyakutai Jizouson**, 100 statues of Buddha that have been here for several hundred years.
Free • 24h

3) The Water Lounge
A secluded space where you can relax and enjoy the views in complete calm. The 14-seat lounge faces a blue water basin, creating a shimmering water surface in front of you as you chill on the cushioned chairs. Purchase an item from **Katsuragi Coffee** to gain entrance for 30 minutes. Most popular are the colorful non-alcoholic cocktails. Hold one up from the lounge for the ultimate Instagram pic!
Free • 9am-5pm

4) Fujimi No Ashiyu
Soak your feet in the footbath and get a different angle over the surroundings. Towels available from staff if you need them.
Free • 9am-4:30pm

5) Saezuri Observation Deck
There are in fact multiple routes up and down from the ropeway to the observation deck, all of which are easy on the feet and take only a few minutes. It's best to take the Sancho-tenbo route up, as this takes you past all the above spots, then return on Kanogawa River route, for views of that to the south. All the routes meet up at the main boardwalk, which heads though a serene tunnel of trees.

Your reward at the top is the Saezuri Observation Deck, with views in the opposite direction of Mount Fuji, including the Amigi Pass, Mount Omuro and Kano River.

Recommended meal spot
Katsuragi Saryo offers similar views to the Water Lounge, but has a menu of light meals. Suruga Bay delicacies are the key here, such as mixed tempura udon, whitebait rice bowls and tricolor dango (sweet dumplings).
Meals from 1000 yen • 9am-5pm

Making our way up!

Top walks for your interests

Most popular – great for tourists new to Tokyo

1) Shibuya to Harajuku (p8)
It would almost be considered a crime to come to Japan and not visit these two areas. They both offer a fascinating insight into Japanese youth culture, and countless photo opportunities.

2) Odaiba (p14)
This walk passes some of Tokyo's most entertaining, and newest, attractions, such as Toyosu Market and the Rainbow bridge, plus some huge shopping and entertainment complexes.

3) Tokyo Station (p16)
The station and surroundings are packed with activities for those that have an afternoon or morning available, from character and mascot shopping to a Japanese noodle street.

4) Akihabara (p36)
Japan's otaku (geek) heartland. Come here to try out the world famous maid and cosplay cafes, dive into all the figurine and gaming shops, or get some tax-free electronics. Many repeat foreign tourists come here every time they visit Tokyo.

5) Enoshima (p78)
Whenever a friend comes to Japan, this is where the locals often take them. The small island is packed with temples, shrines and other tourist hotspots, and is very walkable.

Cherry blossoms (sakura)

First bloom is usually around 22nd March, while full bloom is around 30th March, but as it changes every year do check the official forecast beforehand at jwa.or.jp/english.

1) Ueno (p34)
Ueno Park, the biggest park in Tokyo for cherry blossoms, is many people's number one sakura spot. It can get super busy, but all the small stalls selling cheap food are a real plus.

2) Asakusa (p12)
Along Sumida River in Asakusa is truly amazing. A fun, party atmosphere fills Sumida Park, which has a varied selection of cherry blossom trees.

3) Meguro River (p50)
This long, winding river is the coolest place to see the cherry blossoms, as it's lined with hip cafes and clothing shops. Come at night with a beer or two from a convenience store.

4) Imperial Palace East Garden (p49)
It's well worth walking around the palace, in particular outside the British embassy, near Hanzomon on the Hanzomon Line. You can also rent a boat to row along the petal-filled moat.

5) Roppongi (p44)
Come to Roppongi Sakura-zaka, just south of the Tsutaya bookstore. Best in the evenings, when it's all lit up, and another perfect spot to get a selfie!

Autumn leaves (kouyou)

1) Harajuku (p9) – best mid-November to early December
Located near Harajuku Station, at the end of the Shibuya to Harajuku walk, Yoyogi Park has a huge gingko forest. The park is a popular spot for both locals and foreign tourists to hang out, and a safe bet for seeing the autumn colors.

2) Showa Kinen Park (p64) – best mid-November
Absolutely stunning place to see the golden leaves. It begins with a 300-meter trail lined with ginkgo trees, but you'll see even more if you pick up a rental bicycle and explore the rest of this ginormous park.

3) Shinjuku to Akasaka (p22) – best late November to early December
At the midpoint of this walk you'll come across Jingu Gaien Ginkgo Avenue. Not many sights can rival the 146 monstrously tall gingko trees, with the royal guesthouse in the background.

Shopping

1) Ginza (p46)
All the best high-end brands, from Gucci to Hermes, plus major stores from the likes of Uniqlo and Muji. All the main Tokyo department store chains have a branch here, and they all offer tax-free shopping for foreign tourists.

2) Sugamo (p42)
Join the local grannies at their favorite shopping street in Sugamo. Prices are cheaper than more modern shopping streets, and it has a wonderfully down-to-earth atmosphere.

3) Daikanyama (p26)
If you are looking for more independent clothing and souvenir shops, Daikanyama is a better bet. This hip neighborhood also has plenty of posh cafes to relax in, when you need a break from all that shopping!

Art and museums

1) Roppongi (p44)
Some of the country's best art museums are packed into Roppongi, and this walk goes to the main ones, plus to an art cafe and through an art tunnel!

2) Shibuya (p10)
If you head northwest off Shibuya's main shopping streets, you'll come across a neighborhood with some relatively unknown museums and art galleries. Combine this with the artsy cafes and restaurants, it's a lovely way to spend a sunny afternoon in the city.

3) Karuizawa (p80)
If you are heading north of the city center on the Shinkansen, definitely stop off at Karuizawa. Lots of money has flowed into this area over the years, and what's left is a plethora of interesting art museums, from small ones started by local artists to nationally recognized complexes.

History and culture

1) Yamate (p72)
Yokohama was one of the first places in Japan to open up to foreigners, so visitors to the Yamate area, as well as the Motomachi shopping street, can pop into various former embassies, stately residences and schools, all with a rich history. The culture in this area of Japan is rather unique, possibly only comparable to Nagasaki in the south.

2) Odawara Castle (p89)
Learn about the epic battles, secret ninjas and heroic samurai at the castle closest to Tokyo. There's also a recreated old town and period costume rental, so you can time travel back to ancient times.

3) Hachioji Castle Ruins (p83)
A more off-the-beaten track experience, and another great idea for people that have already visited the main tourist spots in Tokyo. With a history connected to Odawara Castle, there are many stories of deadly battles, and the warrior culture that they inspired.

Day hikes

1) Mount Oyama (p85)
With a combination of tourist conveniences, such as frequent buses and a cable car, and not having the crowds of better known mountains like Mount Takao, Oyama is a perfect blend. It has a few ways to get up and down too, so you can easily customize to your ability.

2) Mount Nokogiri (p88)
It takes a bit of time to get to, but this mountain has some of the most Instagrammable spots in Kanto, so it's well worth the climb up.

3) Takinoo Path (p74)
Venture to some of Nikko's forgotten World Heritage sites, as well as the ones tourists know about, via this ancient path. The hiking sections are through mysterious forests, via moss filled stone paths dotted with religious artifacts.

Long cycling rides

1) Tamagawa River (p56)
The classic Tokyo river cycling ride. It's not wall upon wall of tourist attractions, but mile upon mile of mostly flat cycling paths from the west of Tokyo, all the way to near Haneda Airport. It's very customizable too, and it's easy to finish early or continue all the way to/from the sea.

2) Shakujii River (p67)
Not at all as famous as other cycling spots, but one of the quieter ones. Shakujii River winds its way around the northern suburbs of Tokyo, and ends up at either a traditional shopping street or a hot spring (if you want to do a really long ride).

3) Kamakura (p76)
You'll see that most visitors here just whizz around on the tram, but cycling along the beaches and around the back streets is arguably a better way to see the real Kamakura.

Festival and events calendar

Here is a list of some of the best matsuri (festivals) and events that will work well with the routes in this book. Before going be sure to check for date changes via the official websites, at your hotel or at a tourist information center. For more see the official calendar at gotokyo.org.

January
6th Dezome-shiki: Firemen show off their machines and do various stunts.
Odaiba (p14)

February
3rd Senso-ji Setsubun: Ancient festival that involves throwing soybeans at family members dressed in demon masks, to drive out bad luck and bring good fortune. People flock to Senso-ji to chant away the demons as well.
Asakusa (p12) • senso-ji.jp
Early February Chinese Lunar New Year: Paper lanterns, bright LED lights and two dragons dancing through the streets of Chinatown.
Chinatown, Yokohama (p70) • chinatown.or.jp
From mid-February Ume Matsuri: Amazing plum festival at Yushima Tenmangu Shrine.
Yushima Tenjin, Ueno (p34) • yushimatenjin.or.jp (Japanese only)

March
The cherry blossoms are out! The liveliest spot is the Sakura Festival on the Meguro River (p50), but also check my recommendations for the best spots (p92).

April
Second to third Sundays Kamakura Festival: Ritual dance performances based on the samurai of medieval Japan.
Kamakura (p76) • trip-kamakura.com/site/kamakura-matsuri

May
The Saturday and Sunday closest to May 15th Kanda Matsuri: One of Tokyo's top three festivals, it'll blow your socks off. It has it all, from massive floats to street food.
Kanda, near Akihabara (p36) • kandamyoujin.or.jp/kandamatsuri
18th Shunki Reitaisai: Grand procession of 1,000 'samurai warriors' through the town.
Nikko (p74)
Third Sunday and preceding Friday and Saturday Asakusa Sanja Matsuri: Amazing portable shrines are paraded throughout the town. Mind-blowing stuff.
Asakusa (p12) • asakusajinja.jp/sanjamatsuri
Late May Fussa Friendship Festival: Aircrafts from the Yokota base are put on display, with live music and plenty of food vendors.
Fussa (p66) • yokota.af.mil/Friendship-Festival
Closest weekend to May 28th Hanazono Shrine Grand Festival: Featuring ceremonial rites and dances, plus some cheap food stalls. On Sunday, a huge 1.5 ton portable shrine (mikoshi) is taken on a tour of the surrounding neighborhoods.
Shinjuku (p18)

June

Mid-June Sanno Matsuri: Another big festival in Tokyo, with a splendid procession of miniature shrines, floats and colorfully dressed dancers.
Hie Shrine, near the Diet Building (p38) • tenkamatsuri.jp
Mid-June Fussa Firefly Festival: See fireflies dancing about at night, along the banks of Kita-Asakawa River, creating an almost fantasy-style spectacle.
Hotaru Park and Ome Bridge, in Fussa (p66) • fussakanko.jp (Japanese only)

July

Last Saturday Sumida River Fireworks: Tokyo's biggest and best fireworks display.
Asakusa (p12) • sumidagawa-hanabi.com

August

All month long Enoshima Toro Lantern Festival: 1,000 lanterns are put out to illuminate the island's tourist spots. On the first Saturday and Sunday around 5,000 bamboo lanterns fill up Ryukoji Temple, which is not far from the walking path in this book.
Enoshima (p78) • travelenoshima.jp/festival/lantern.html
Last weekend Omotesando Genki Festival: More than 5,000 energetic dancers from 100-plus groups performing along Harajuku's main street.
Harajuku (p9) • super-yosakoi.tokyo

September

14-16th Reitaisai: Traditional horseback archery display and contest.
Kamakura (p76)
Late September Tokyo Game Show: The biggest videogame expo in Japan, where you'll be able to play games before release, see exciting new announcements and maybe meet a few stars.
Makuhari Messe, on the way to Chiba (p88) • expo.nikkeibp.co.jp/tgs

October

Late October to mid-November Chrysanthemum Festival: More than 1500 varieties of flowers on display, from Bonsai to colorful cascades.
Takahata-Fudoson Temple, near Hachioji (p83)
Mid-October Tokyo Yosakoi Festival: Countless groups showing off this energetic, yet very traditional form of Japanese dance.
Ikebukuro (p40)

November

Late September Hachioji Ginkgo Festival: Beautiful rows of golden ginkgo trees line Koshu Road. Pick up a 'tsuku tegata', a wooden block that was used as a transit pass in olden times, and explore the ancient checkpoints and bazaar.
Koshu Road, near Hachioji station, on the way to Hachioji Castle Ruins (p83) • ichou-festa.org

December

Christmas and New Year The best winter illuminations can be found at Lights Terrace City, Shinjuku (p18), Naka-Dori Avenue, near Tokyo Station (p16) and Roppongi Midtown (p44).

Index

10 YEN Pancake, 10
100-yen shops
    Can Do, 37
    Daiso, 20
47 Ronin, 24
Airport Garden, 30
airport transportation, 6
Akasaka, 22, 38
Akiba Cultures Zone, 37
Akihabara, 36
Akihabara Gamers, 36
Akihabara Junk Street, 37
Animate, 40
Ao Terrace, 91
Aoyama Cemetery, 38
Arakawa Amusement Park, 32
art and museums (best of), 93
art museums & galleries
    21_21 Design Sight, 45
    Asakura Museum of Sculpture, 35
    Gallery TOM, 11
    Ginza Graphic Gallery, 48
    Karuizawa New Art Museum, 80
    Mitsubishi Ichigokan Museum, 17
    Mori Art Museum, 45
    Museum of Contemporary Art, 61
    National Art Center, 39
    National Museum of Modern Art, 50
    Nezu Museum, 38
    Ota Memorial Museum of Art, 9
    Petit Museum, 80
    Roppongi Tunnel, 45
    Shoto Museum of Art, 11
    Sompo Museum of Art, 19
    Toguri Museum, 11
    Wakita Museum of Art, 80
    WHAT Museum, 28
Asakusa, 12
Asakusa Hanayashiki, 13
Asakusa Line, 24, 47
autumn leaves (best of), 93
Barahi Foods & Spice Center, 21
Base Side street, 66
bento, 16, 19, 41, 48, 54, 61, 77, 89
Benzaiten Nakamise Street, 78
Berrick Hall, 73
Big Mama, 66
Bluff No.18, 73
Bond Street, 29
breweries
    Ishikawa Sake Brewery, 57
    Nogi-jinja Shrine, 39
    Spring Valley Brewery Tokyo, 27
bridges
    Kiyosu Bridge, 61
    Megane Bridge, 82
    Nikko Bridge, 66
    Rainbow Bridge, 15
    Shinagawa Bridge, 51
    Shinkyo Bridge, 75
    Tamagawa Sky Bridge, 31
British House, 72
Bunkamura Dori Street, 10
cafes
    2D Cafe, 21
    Akihabara maid cafes, 37
    Anakuma, 9
    Bake Cheese Tart, 17
    BAKE the SHOP, 53
    Blue Seal, 67
    Bvlgari Ginza Bar, 48
    Cafe Racines Farm, 41
    Camelish, 46
    Chaya Sakura-ya, 87
    Croquette Korokya, 43
    Daikokudo, 57
    Eggs 'n Things, 15
    Enokitei, 73
    Flipper's, 52
    Goku Tea House, 71
    Harry Potter Cafe, 39
    Hongu Cafe, 76
    I'm Donut, 51
    Joseki Tea House, 85
    Katsuragi Coffee, 91
    Kibiya Bakery, 77
    Kosoan, 53
    Maidreamin, 11
    Mini Mini, 83
    Natural Cafeína, 81
    Nezu Café, 39
    Princi, 27
    Raku Ishihama Teahouse, 33
    Royal Garden Cafe Aoyama, 23

Sepia, 63
Starbucks, 35
Sukemasa Coffee, 13
Sunmelt Coffee, 69
Swallowtail Cafe, 41
Sweets Paradise, 9
The Sunrise Shack, 77
Trex Kawasaki River Café, 31
Truffle Bakery, 61
Tully's Coffee, 25
Umitama Do, 79
WHAT Cafe, 29
Yamamoto-tei, 63
Calbee, 16
Cape Inamuragasaki, 77
castles
    Hachioji Castle, 84
    Odawara Castle, 90
    Takiyama Castle Ruins, 57
Cat Street, 9
cherry blossoms (best of), 92
Chiyoda Line, 24, 38, 44
Chocolate Bank, 77
Chofu, 55
Chuo Line, 66
Chuo-dori, 19
churches
    Karuizawa Shaw Memorial Church, 81
    St. Paul's Catholic Church, 81
    Yokohama Christ Church, 73
curry, 31, 46, 51, 61, 65, 77, 81, 83
Cyberspace Shibuya, 8
cycling rides (best of), 94
Daikanyama, 26
Daily Chico, 54
Denboin-dori Street, 13
department stores
    atré Shinagawa, 29
    Don Quijote, 21, 36
    Ginza Six, 47
    GRANSTA, 16
    Harajuku Alta, 9
    Jiyugaoka Depart, 52
    Keio Department Store, 18
    LOAX, 37
    Matsuya Ginza, 48
    MEGA Don Quijote, 10
    Minaka Odawara, 90
    Mitsukoshi, 47
    Omotesando Hills, 9

Seibu Ikebukuro, 41
Shibuya 109, 10
Shibuya Loft, 11
Shibuya Parco, 8
Yokohama Daisekai, 71
Diplomat's House, 73
Donguri Kyowakoku, 41
Dragon Quest, 37
Ehrismann Mansion, 73
electronics stores
    Bic Camera, 36, 40
    Fujiya Camera, 54
    Yamada Denki, 40
    Yodobashi Camera, 18
Enoshima, 78
Enoshima Electric Railway, 76, 78
Enoshima Escar, 78
Enoshima Kamakura Free Pass, 5
Enoshima Sea Candle, 79
Evangelion Store, 41
festivals, 95
First Avenue, 16, 17
foot spas
    Footbath Skydeck, 31
    Fujimi No Ashiyu, 91
    Minaka Odawara, 90
Former Kumanotaira Station, 82
Fukutoshin Line, 8, 40
Fussa, 66
Fussa American House, 66
Gachapon Hall, 37
Gallery on the Hill, 26
gaming arcades, 36
Gaochi, 54
gardens and parks
    Aquatic Botanical Gardens, 55
    Chidorigafuchi Park, 49
    Daiba Park, 15
    East Gardens of the Imperial Palace, 49
    French Hill Park, 72
    Futako-Tamagawa Park, 57
    Hibiya Park, 25
    Hotel New Otani Japanese Garden, 23
    Ikegami Plum Garden, 59
    Jindai Botanical Gardens, 55
    Kiyosumi Gardens, 60
    Machida Squirrel Garden, 69
    Minami-ikebukuro Park, 41
    Miyashita Park, 8
    Mukojima-Hyakkaen Gardens, 33

Otonashi Momiji Green Park, 67
Otonashi Sakura Green Park, 67
Saikiyama Green Hill, 59
Samuel Cocking Garden, 79
Shikisai no Mori, 68
Shinjuku Central Park, 19
Shinjuku Gyoen National Garden, 22
Tamagawadai Park, 56
Ueno Park, 34
Usui Pass Railway Heritage Park, 83
Yakushiike Park, 68
Yamate Italian Garden, 73
Genbumon Gate, 70
Gindako, 54
Ginza Line, 8, 34, 38, 46, 47, 48, 81, 93
Ginza Place, 47
Gotanda Fureai Waterside Plaza, 51
Green Nasco, 21
gyudon, 59, 77
Hachiko, 10
Hachiman-dori Street, 27
Hachioji, 83
Haijima, 56
Haikara Yokocho, 62
Haneda Airport, 30
Haneda Innovation City, 31
Hanzomon Line, 8, 38, 60
Harajuku, 8
Hello Cycling, 7
Hibiya Line, 24, 25, 34, 44, 47
hikes (best of), 94
Hillside Terrace, 26
Historic Mikasa Hotel, 81
history and culture (best of), 94
Hollywood Ranch Market, 26
Hoppy Street, 13
hot springs
    Akishima Onsen Yuranosato, 57
    Inamuragasaki Onsen, 77
    Kitashinagawa Spa Tenjinyu, 28
    Mannenyu, 20
    Niwa-no-yu, 67
    Sakura Onsen, 43
    Spa Izumi, 30
    Sugamo Yu, 43
    Toge No Yu, 82
Hotteok, 21
Hyakushaku Kannon, 88
Hyakutai Jizouson, 91
IC cards, 6

Ichiba Dori Shopping Street, 71
Ikebukuro, 40
Islam Alley, 21
Itabashi, 67
Itoya, 48
Iwaya Caves, 79
Izu Peninsula, 91
Izu-Hakone Line, 91
Izunokuni Panorama Park Ropeway, 91
Janpara, 36
Japan National Stadium, 22
Jigoku Nozoki, 88
Jindaiji Pet Cemetery, 55
Jingu Gaien Ginkgo Avenue, 23
Jiyugaoka, 52
Kabukiza, 47
Kamakura, 76
Kamawanu, 27
Kappabashi Dougu Street, 13
Karuizawa, 80
Karuizawa Prince Shopping Plaza, 81
Karuizawa's Apt Road, 82
Kawasaki, 56
K-Books, 41
Keihin-Tohoku Line, 24, 32, 58, 67
Keikyu Line, 6, 28
Keio Line, 55, 84
Keisei-Kanamachi Line, 62
Kintaro-ame, 42
Kita-Shinagawa Shopping Street, 28
Koma Sando, 86
Kome To Circus, 8
Korea Town, 20
Koto City, 60
Kotobukiya, 37
Kumoba Pond, 81
Kyu Asakura House, 26
Kyukyodo, 48
La Vita, 53
Log Road Daikanyama, 27
Lost in Translation, 19
Lotus Pond, 68
LOVE sculpture, 19
Mandarake, 37, 41, 54
Manpei Hotel, 80
map legend, 4
markets
    Adachi Fisheries Market, 32
    Nogi-jinja Shrine, 39
    Shinjuku Central Park, 19

Toyosu Market, 14
Maruji, 43
Marunouchi Brick Square, 17
Marunouchi Building, 17
Marunouchi Ekimae Square, 17
Marunouchi Line, 16, 17, 18, 22, 24, 40
Mega Tokyo, 41
Meguro River, 50
Minato City, 24
Mita Line, 67
Monzen-nakacho, 61
Most popular routes, 92
Motomachi Shopping Street, 71
Mount Nokogiri Ropeway, 88
Mount Oyama, 85
MUJI Ginza Flagship Store, 48
museums
    Drum Museum, 13
    Edo Taito Crafts Center, 13
    Fukagawa Edo Museum, 60
    Japan Olympic Museum, 23
    Manpukuji, 59
    Meiji Memorial Museum, 23
    Nikon Museum, 29
    Ota City Local History Museum, 59
    Poop Museum Tokyo, 14
    Ryushi Memorial Museum, 59
    Shibamata Toy Museum, 62
    Tokyo National Museum, 35
    Tora-san Museum, 63
    Trick Art Museum, 71
    Yamate Archives Museum, 73
Naka-Dori Avenue, 17
Naka-Meguro Park, 50
Nakamise-dori Street, 12
Nakano, 54
Nakano Broadway, 54
Nakano Sun Mall, 54
Namboku Line, 32
Namjatown, 41
National Diet Building, 39
New York Bar, 19
Nikko, 74
Nintendo Tokyo, 8
Nippori, 34
Nishi-Shinjuku, 18
NTT Docomo Bike Share, 7
Odaiba, 14
Odakyu Enoshima Line, 78
Odakyu Line, 68, 89

Odawara, 89
oden, 90
Oedo Line, 18, 60
Oji, 32, 67
okonomiyaki, 13
Old Karuizawa Ginza Street, 81
Old Maruyama Substation, 82
Old Nakasendo Street, 67
Ome Line, 64, 66
online maps, 4
Onna-zaka Path, 86
Onoden, 37
opening days, 5
Oshiage, 32
Otoko-zaka, 87
Otome Road, 41
Oyama Afuri Shrine Honsha, 86
Oyama Tofu, 87
Oyama Tozan Cable Car, 86
Park Hyatt Tokyo, 19
Pigment, 29
Pokemon Center, 8, 41
Radio Kaikan, 36
ramen, 15, 17, 41, 54, 57, 85
Refutei, 54
restaurants
    &Burger, 33
    Café 33, 50
    Chicken Mochigome Tangsuyuku, 21
    Demode Diner, 67
    Eggslut, 9
    Fussa No Birugoya, 57
    Fuunji, 19
    Gamaro Gangjung, 21
    Go Go Curry, 31
    Hot Spoon, 51
    Hotto Motto, 77
    Japan Loves Curry, 31
    Kankiro, 87
    Katsuragi Saryo, 91
    Macchan, 21
    Meiji No Yakata, 76
    Mendokoro, 41
    Miso Ga Ichiban, 54
    Mos Burger, 25
    Mototaki, 87
    Museca Times, 35
    Nangman_29, 21
    Nene Chicken, 20
    Ninja Tokyo, 23

Odaiba Takoyaki Museum, 15
Odawara Oden, 90
Old House Cafe Rengetsu, 59
POPO Hotteok, 21
Roast Beef Ono, 37
Sanga Soba & Coffee Stand, 89
Sangosho Moana Makai, 77
Shibuya Yokocho, 9
Shichifuku, 71
Shunya-chan, 85
Sometaro, 13
Spaghetti no Pancho, 37
Spring Valley Brewery Tokyo, 27
Suzu no Ne, 81
T.Y. Harbor, 29
Toge-no-Yu, 83
Tokyo Plaza Ginza, 48
Tokyo Ramen Kokugikan Mai, 15
Tokyo Ramen Street, 17
Tousha, 79
Tsujita Miso no Sho, 17
Tsuru Ton Tan, 46
Washiya, 54
Roppongi, 38, 44
Roppongi Sakura-zaka, 92
Roppongi Tsutaya Books, 45
Saezuri Observation Deck, 91
Saikyo Line, 40
sake, 9, 40, 57, 87
Sarugakucho, 26
Sarutahiko Okami, 43
sashimi, 13
Sengohyaku Rakan, 88
Seoul Ichiba, 20
Shakujii River, 67
Shibamata, 62
Shibuya, 8, 10
Shibuya Center Gai, 8
Shibuya Scramble Crossing, 8
Shinagawa, 28
Shinagawa Intercity, 29
Shinjuku, 22
Shinkansen, 16, 28, 74, 80, 82, 89, 91, 93
shopping (best of), 93
Showa Kinen Park, 64
shrines
    Anamori Inari Shrine, 31
    Benten-do, 13
    Ebara Shrine, 51
    Enoshima Shrine, 79
    Former Anamori Inari Shrine Gate, 31
    Futarasan Shrine, 75
    Hachioji Shrine, 85
    Hie Shrine, 39
    Hongu Shrine, 75
    Hotoku Ninomiya Shrine, 90
    Ishihama-Jinja, 33
    Kannon-do, 75
    Katsuragi Shrine, 91
    Kitano Shrine, 75
    Kumano Shrine, 53
    Mita Hachiman Jinja, 24
    Nogi-jinja Shrine, 39
    Oyama Afuri Shrine, 86
    Takinoo Shrine, 75
    Tamagawa Sengen Shrine, 56
    Tomioka Hachiman Shrine, 61
    Toshogu Shrine, 75
soba, 55, 57, 83, 87, 89
Sobu Line, 20
SoLaDo, 9
Somei Cemetery, 43
Sony Park Mini, 48
Stairway of Success, 25
State Guest House Akasaka Palace, 23
Statue of Liberty, 15
Strawberry Fetish, 9
Sugamo, 42
Sugamo Jizodori Shopping Street, 42
Sunshine Aquarium, 41
Sunshine City, 41
Super Potato, 37
Suruga-ya, 36
sushi, 50, 57, 65
Tachikawa, 64
taco rice, 81
Taishakuten Sando, 62
Takeshita Street, 9
takoyaki, 15, 54
Tama River Cycling Road, 31
Tanzawa-Oyama Freepass, 85
teishoku, 43, 79
temples
    Daibo Hongyoji, 59
    Enoshima Daishi, 79
    Fukagawa Fudoson, 61
    Fukuoji, 69
    Gojukkenbana Muenbotoke Pagoda, 31
    Hasedera Temple, 77
    Honmyoji, 43

Ikegami Honmonji Temple, 58
Jindaiji Temple, 55
Jindaiji Tsukuri Shi, 55
Joshinji Temple, 53
Kenkonzan Nihon-ji Temple, 89
Kongoji Temple, 67
Kotoku-in, 77
Kuan Ti Miao Temple, 71
Manpuku-ji Temple, 76
Oyama Temple, 86
Rinnoji Temple, 76
Ryuko-ji, 76
Sengakuji Temple, 24
Senso-ji, 12
Shibamata Taishakuten, 63
The Big Stone Buddha, 89
Tokyo Mazu Temple, 21
Yatsu Daikannon, 67
Zen-yoji Temple, 56
tempura, 33, 89, 91
Tennozu Isle, 28
The Water Lounge, 91
Today's Special, 53
tofu, 69, 87
Tokiwa Kimon Samurai Centre, 89
Tokyo Character Street, 16
Tokyo City View, 45
Tokyo Imperial Palace, 49
Tokyo Joypolis, 15
Tokyo Metropolitan Building, 19
Tokyo Midtown, 45
Tokyo Okashi Land, 16
Tokyo Skytree, 33
Tokyo Station, 16
Tokyo Subway Ticket, 5
Tokyo Tower, 25
Tokyo Wide Pass, 5

Tokyu Ikegami Line, 58
Tokyu Toyoko Line, 26, 27, 50, 52, 56, 70, 72
Tom Sawyer Workshop, 66
Toranomon Hills, 25
Toshimaen, 67
Tozai Line, 60
Train passes, 5
T-Site, 27
tsukemen, 19, 54
Tsukuba Express Line, 12
Tsurumi River, 68
udon, 46, 87, 91
Ueno, 34
Ueno Zoo, 34
Unicorn Gundam Statue, 15
Uniqlo Ginza, 48
useful apps, 5
Usui Lake, 82
Usui Sekisho Checkpoint, 83
Utsunomiya Line, 74
Vermicular, 26
Yagiri-no-watashi, 63
yakitori, 13, 48
Yamanote Line, 8, 16, 18, 20, 24, 28, 36, 40, 42, 47
Yamate, 72
Yamate Hondori Street, 73
Yanaka Cemetery, 35
Yanaka Ginza, 35
Yokohama, 70
Yokohama Chocolate Factory, 71
Yokohama Marine Tower, 71
Yokota Base Gate No. 5, 66
Yurakucho, 48
Yurakucho Line, 40, 47
Yurikamome Line, 14

Many thanks for reading

Help spread the word

Please help this self-published book by writing a review online, sharing the book on Facebook or Instagram, or telling a friend. As this is a self-funded indie project, it would be super useful and very much appreciated!

Like or follow me to get the latest tips and deals

 www.supercheapjapan.com

 @SuperCheapJapan

 @SuperCheapJapan

#TokyoOutdoors

Contact me

If you have any questions or comments, please contact me at matt@supercheapjapan.com, or message me on Instagram (www.instagram.com/supercheapjapan) or Facebook (www.facebook.com/supercheapjapan).

@SUPERCHEAPJAPAN

Acknowledgements

Additional Tokyo pictures © TCVB
Maps made using MapOSMatic
Map data from OpenStreetMap (openstreetmap.org/copyright), available under the Open Database License
Dudva, Christophe95, 663highland, MaedaAkihiko CC BY-SA 4.0 via Wikimedia Commons

Useful Japanese for traveling

Essential phrases
Do you speak English? - Eigo ga hanasemas ka? / 英語が話せますか？
Hello! - Konnichiwa! / こんにちは！
Yes - Hai / はい
No - Iie / いいえ
Thank you - Arigatou / ありがとう
Sorry - Sumimasen / すみません
I don't understand - Wakarimasen / わかりません
Please write down (e.g. number, price) - Kaite kudasai / かいてください
Where is the _? - _ wa doko des ka? / _はどこですか？
Insert the following above to ask for directions:
Toilet = Toire / トイレ ・ Train station = Eki / えき ・ Subway station = Chikatetsu / ちかてつ

Shopping
How much is this? - Ikura des ka? / いくらですか？
Do you have _? - _ arimas ka? / _ありますか？

Getting food and drink
Do you have an English menu? - Eigo no menyu wa arimas ka? / 英語のメニューはありますか？
I'd like _ please - _ o kudasai / _をください
That please - Kore o kudasai / これをください (point at the item)
Water please (save on drinks) - Omizu o kudasai / お水をください
Refill please! (use if free refills available) - Okawari! / おかわり！
Takeout please - Teiku-auto de / テイクアウトで
Eat-in please - Eeto-in de / イートインで
Is there a cover or table charge? - Chaaji arimas ka? / チャージありますか？

Traveling around
Please tell me when we get to _. (good for buses/trains with no English signs) - _ ni tsuku toki ni oshiete kudasai / _に着くときに教えてください

Numbers
0 - zero / 〇
1 - ichi / 一
2 - ni / 二
3 - san / 三
4 - shi/yon / 四
5 - go / 五
6 - roku / 六
7 - shichi/nana / 七
8 - hatchi / 八
9 - kyū / 九
10 - jū / 十
11 - jū-ichi (sound for 10, then sound for 1) / 十一 (so 12 is 'jū-ni', 13 is 'jū-san' etc)

Other books written by Matthew Baxter

Super Cheap Japan: Budget Travel in Tokyo, Kyoto, Osaka, Nara, Hiroshima and Surrounding Areas (ISBN: 978-1-9196315-0-9)
The ultimate budget travel guide to a cheap holiday in Honshu (Japan's main island). Go shopping for $4 clothes in Tokyo, enjoy inexpensive hikes in Nikko, or visit Kyoto's beautiful shrines and gardens on the cheap; all with this super helpful guide.

Super Cheap Hokkaido: The Ultimate Budget Travel Guide to Sapporo and the Hokkaido Prefecture (ISBN: 978-1-9131140-0-8)
The perfect companion for a budget holiday to Sapporo and the surrounding Hokkaido prefecture. A follow-up to the bestselling Super Cheap Japan guidebook, this book will show you exactly how, where and when you can save money on your trip.

Super Cheap New Zealand: The Ultimate Travel Guide for Budget Travelers, Backpackers, Campers, Students and Families (ISBN: 978-1-913114-05-3)
The ultimate budget travel guide to New Zealand, full of the most useful, up-to-date information for a cheap holiday in this amazing country.

About the Author

Tokyo Outdoors was written by Matthew Baxter, a British travel author who has lived in and out of Japan for many years. Having traveled across the country for several years, without much money, he has built up an extensive knowledge of budget travel in the Land of the Rising Sun. He now writes professionally for several websites and publications, such as the Japan National Tourist Association, Japan Visitor and All About Japan.

www.ingramcontent.com/pod-product-compliance
Lightning Source LLC
Chambersburg PA
CBHW052200110526
44591CB00012B/2016